Seventeen-Point

MIRACLE

ISBN 978-1-936208-86-9

Cover design: Megan Yoder

Text layout design: Felicia Kern

Third printing: May 2019

For more information about Christian Aid Ministries, see page 183.

Published by:
TGS International
P.O. Box 355
Berlin, Ohio 44610 USA
Phone: 330·893·4828
Fax: 330·893·2305
www.tgsinternational.com

TGS001952

Seventeen-Ounce
MIRACLE

RACHAEL LOFGREN

Table of Contents

1. A Day to Stay Inside 11
2. Decisions 19
3. Miracle in the Night 29
4. Reality Hits 37
5. His Hands and Feet 43
6. It Can't Be Done! 51
7. The Peace Speaker 57
8. A Big God 65
9. Settling In 71
10. Precious Firsts 79
11. Reaching Out 85
12. No Matter What, God Loves Me! 93
13. Emergency Surgery 101
14. Dolphins and Family Prayers 109
15. Milestones 117
16. Valley of the Shadow 123

17. A Place of Tears 131
18. Politicians and Elephants 137
19. Weekend Diversion 143
20. Bulldog With a Bone 149
21. Trip of the Lost Luggage 155
22. Setbacks 161
23. The Long-Awaited Day 169
24. The Continuing Miracle 175
    Epilogue 179
    About the Author 181

Dedication

✿ With love to Mom, my closest earthly friend.

Acknowledgments

A sincere and heartfelt thank you to all those who made the writing of this book possible:

❀ To Galen, Esther, and your family, for the joy it was to be in your home and hear your story, and for your patience and willingness to share information throughout the writing process.

❀ To my personal proofreading and editing team, Patti Lofgren, Barb Smith, and Judi B., who shared so intimately in the process of this book.

❀ To my family and church family. Your support is such a blessing!

❀ To my editors at CAM, for all you did to prepare this book for publication.

❀ Above all, to the Author and Finisher of our faith. To Him alone be all the glory.

A Day to Stay Inside

—Esther

The damp, chilly air flowed over me as I was carried through the hospital's double glass doors. I shivered despite the blanket covering me. Beyond the roof of the carport, I caught sight of the sullen gray of a weepy February sky. One of the burly paramedics caught my eye and smiled. "We'll have you inside in just a moment." His cheerfulness relaxed me. "Ready, Devon?" He glanced at his partner, who nodded. "In we go."

I smiled a little as they lifted my stretcher into the back of the ambulance waiting to transfer me from Elizabethtown, Kentucky, to Louisville. "It does seem like a good day to stay inside," I commented.

The paramedic's jovial face grew sober. "I just hope this baby stays inside too. I can't say I feel too eager to be practicing any obstetrics on the way to Louisville."

Devon nodded in agreement. "I'm just glad I'm driving.

Didn't you say you've delivered a baby once before, Bill?"

"Yeah, once. It was on an ambulance too. But it wasn't something I want to do again."

"I guess not," Devon agreed heartily. "But if this baby does decide to come, you tell me. I'll put the lights and sirens on and we'll get there fast."

"Any excuse to speed, huh?" Bill chuckled.

My mind wandered from their banter as I felt another contraction coming on. They weren't hard, but they were coming steadily. I shifted uncomfortably on the stretcher.

At our first doctor's appointment two weeks ago, everything had appeared normal on the ultrasound. We found out we were expecting another girl, and both Galen and I were excited. This would make three precious girls in our family.

In the doctor's office, I had mentioned that I had experienced some sharp pains off and on for the past week, but the doctor was having a busy day and seemed in a hurry. "I don't think it's anything to worry much about," he told me. "Let me know if there are any changes." I didn't bother to expound on my vague explanation and thought little more about the incident.

Then last night we had hosted a group of friends for supper. I should have known it would be too much for me. But I had felt so good, and everything had gone well. After the rush was over and all the guests were gone, however, I regretted my decision. My whole body ached. I could hardly put one foot in front of the other. Feeling terrible, I sank into the recliner in our office and pulled a pregnancy book from the bookshelf.

Scanning the pages, my mind rebelled against what I was reading. I pictured a dismal hospital room and saw myself lying flat on my back for days, time dragging endlessly. *I am not going on bed rest. My girls need me,* I thought desperately. *God, please just let this be a normal pregnancy.*

Galen stuck his head through the doorway and asked if I was all right.

I looked up. "I feel terrible. But I'm hoping I can just sleep this off." I caught a trace of concern in his eyes, and my own filled with tears. "I don't want to go on bed rest. The girls need me, Galen."

"It'll be okay, Esther. Let's pray about it and go to bed. Hopefully you'll feel better by morning." He took my hand. As he prayed, my weary heart was comforted. We were in God's hands, and that was a safe place to be.

I slept restlessly at first, but toward morning I fell into a heavy sleep, only to awaken a few hours later to Darika whimpering in her crib. Pushing back the covers, I groggily headed for the kitchen to fix her a bottle. As I stood by the sink, I suddenly felt that I was leaking fluid. "Galen, I need help!" I called urgently down the hallway.

"I think you'd better call your doctor and ask him what to do," Galen said as he took the bottle from me. "I'll feed Darika and get Alisha up and dressed." I hurried to the phone and dialed the number.

The nurse I spoke with conferred with the doctor and then told me briskly, "Don't even come to the clinic. The doctor said you should just go straight to the hospital. I'll call them and let them know you're coming." I thanked her and hung up.

"Galen, the doctor says we should just go straight to the

hospital," I relayed to him.

"Okay, I'll do the chores fast," he said. "Maybe we can leave the girls with your dad and mom. I'll call them on the way down to the barns and see. Are you up to getting Alisha's breakfast?" I nodded as he finished zipping up her dress. "All right then, I'll go check the chickens and be back soon."

My mind swam with all the things I'd need to pack as I set a bowl of Cheerios in front of our two-year-old. "Alisha, here's your breakfast." She looked up into my face and smiled, and I couldn't help but stop for a moment. I stroked her blond hair back from her forehead and bent down to kiss her. "Is my Alisha ready for a big day?" She nodded, and I left her to eat her breakfast while I packed.

When Galen and I got married, we had high hopes that God would bless us with children. When we found out we were expecting our first child, our hearts sang. But we never held our first baby in our arms, because God chose to take our little one home to be with Him.

For the first four years of marriage, each successive pregnancy brought new hope and ended in miscarriage. Finally we asked for anointing and prayer for healing, and we consulted another doctor. I had one more miscarriage before I was finally able to carry a baby to term. Alisha arrived on a bright day in May. She was a perfect fifth anniversary gift. We couldn't have been happier. But another little one joined our treasures in heaven before Darika arrived two years later.

Several months after Darika was born, I found out I was

expecting again. I felt slightly overwhelmed at first, since Darika was still so little and my body was just recovering from my last pregnancy. Nevertheless, our hearts rejoiced at the thought of another little one, and we knew God had given us this opportunity for a reason.

Galen finished the chores quickly, and we piled into our minivan. Just as we were leaving the house, I started cramping. After dropping the girls off and driving for forty-five minutes, we arrived at the hospital in Elizabethtown. They were expecting us and checked us in with few questions. As I waited in the observation room in the maternity ward, I wondered how this would all end. By then my contractions were coming more frequently. The nurse had informed us that I was dilated to three centimeters.

Soon a doctor entered the room. "Hello, I'm Dr. Myna." She shook our hands briskly and flipped open a folder. "So you're Esther Lengacher?" I nodded, smiling at the obvious question. "And you must be her husband." She gave Galen a quick nod and a smile. "We've been informed of your condition, and your doctor also sent us your history. I'm going to do a quick exam, and we'll go from there."

As she worked she continued, "We don't usually handle very premature babies in the hospital here in Elizabethtown— especially when it's this early. We just wouldn't feel confident trying to deal with a 22-weeker." She paused as she slipped her stethoscope into her ears. I looked at Galen. He smiled at me, trying to calm my trepidation. I knew that getting uptight would just make things worse, so I relaxed as best as I could and waited for the doctor's verdict.

"You'll need to transfer to Louisville," Dr. Myna said with finality. My heart skipped a beat. People only went to Louisville if their case was critical. I glanced at Galen.

"It doesn't look as though we have any other options at this point." He shrugged and turned to the doctor. "We'll go."

"Okay, we'll call for an ambulance." Dr. Myna took a syringe from a nearby table. "This is a steroid shot to speed up the lung development of the fetus," she explained briefly. "We want to give the baby every chance we can." After she finished giving me the injection, she said, "I wish you the best of luck." With another professional smile, she was gone.

I turned to Galen and sighed.

"Tired?" he asked gently, taking my hand.

"I guess I'm more thirsty than anything." I swallowed hard and ran my tongue over the roof of my mouth. It felt terribly parched. "Uncomfortable too. I wonder if elevating my feet really does anything."

"I wondered that myself," Galen responded. "I suppose it makes sense to keep your head down and your feet up if gravity comes into play at all. I'll ask if they can get you something to drink."

Just then a nurse walked in the door. Galen approached her. "Could Esther have something to drink?" he asked. "She's been without water for several hours now and is feeling very thirsty."

The nurse smiled apologetically. "I'm sorry. We can't give you anything before transport."

"What about ice chips?"

"No, we generally don't give anything at all right before transport. I'm sorry." She left the room and Galen turned back to me, his eyes sympathetic.

Time passed slowly as we waited for the ambulance. Realizing with stark clarity the urgency of our situation, we felt the need to hurry. But there was nothing to do but wait. My mind rested briefly on the girls. It was such a blessing to know they were in good hands. I glanced at Galen. Though I could sense his impatience to be on our way, there was no fear in his demeanor. I marveled at how calm I felt.

I looked up as another nurse entered our room. I wondered if she had come to notify us that the ambulance had come. She wasn't in a hurry, though, and I sensed her mission was more than medical.

"Hello, my name is Joyce." Her round face was cheerful and her eyes smiled down at me. "So you're transferring to Louisville?" It was more of a statement than a question, but the compassion in her voice brought a lump to my throat. She sat down gently on the edge of the bed.

"I just wanted to let you know that I hope everything goes well for you folks." She touched my shoulder. "This is not impossible. I had a sister who was born very prematurely, and she made it just fine. She was blind, but even that was something we were able to work through. And that was years ago. With modern technology they are able to do amazing things even with very premature infants. I'm sure you folks will be all right." She reached out and gave me a strong hug. "Hang in there, Esther. Don't give up hope." My eyes misted as I watched her go. What a sweet message of hope when we needed it most!

Several moments later the ambulance crew arrived. Galen planned to follow in our vehicle. When he left to bring our van around to the loading dock, I felt alone without his steady presence. But the jovial paramedics helped me calm down.

Now as they loaded me into the ambulance, they joked back and forth. The cold air and gas fumes mingled around me, making my already parched throat feel tight.

As they stabilized me in preparation for transport, Galen pulled up beside us in our minivan. He appeared around the side of the ambulance, and I heard him ask the men if it would be okay if he said goodbye to me.

"Sure, come on up," Bill invited. "She'll be well taken care of."

Galen climbed in beside me. For an instant our eyes met. Then with a quick kiss he was gone, and the back doors of the ambulance were shut. I settled down for the long ride ahead and hoped the baby would wait at least until we got there.

As we drove, Bill and I chatted about our families and our children. His manner was mellow and kind, and I was grateful to be in capable hands. It seemed as if it took forever to reach the interstate, though. Galen called me once, since we both had our cell phones. Bill grinned and pretended to be busy elsewhere.

Galen told me that he had called our minister, James, and asked him to put us on the church prayer hotline. I was grateful. I sensed that God was in control, and I knew He worked through the prayers of His people.

After we ended our call, I turned to Bill. "I'm having another contraction," I said mechanically. I had been instructed to tell him every time I felt a contraction coming on, and it felt rather awkward.

As we turned north on I-65, Devon moved into the fast lane and picked up speed. We cruised toward Louisville, little dreaming just how familiar this route would become in the months ahead.

2 Decisions

—Esther

I tried to swallow to ease the dryness in my throat. My tongue felt thick and raspy against the roof of my mouth. I felt utterly drained, as if I might pass out any moment.

I glanced around at the sterile whiteness and harsh lighting of the large intensive care room. It all seemed so big and strange. Then I caught sight of Galen coming through the doorway. My heartbeat slowed and I smiled feebly as he took my hand.

"Are you all right?" he asked gently. I nodded, just glad he was there.

"For a bit I wasn't sure how I was going to find you in here," he explained. "But after I found a parking spot and headed inside, one of the ambulance crew members saw me passing the tunnel, and he ran over and showed me where they took you in."

Just then a wiry, bald man with an authoritative air

entered the room. Obviously he was the doctor we had been waiting for. He turned to the nursing staff and barked, "Get that magnesium going. Why haven't you started it yet?" As I caught sight of his face, I was taken aback by the sharpness of his stern features, and I felt an instant uncertainty.

My face must have conveyed my inner apprehension. The doctor turned to me with a quick smile. "Don't let my looks bother you. I was up all night." I glanced at Galen, who grinned at me.

Turning to the doctor, I asked, "Could I have something to drink?" My voice was barely a whisper and my throat felt dry and scratchy.

"Sure." Turning to the nurse, he ordered, "Get her something to drink and move her into a normal position. Having her tilted upside-down like that isn't going to help stop anything."

He smiled good-naturedly at Galen, but I could read the weariness in his voice. "By the way, I'm Dr. Perentonio, but everyone calls me Dr. P. I've looked into your case a bit, and I'm not sure what path of action you want to pursue. I'll discuss the options with you."

The nurse moved my bed into a normal position and handed me a cup of water. The cool liquid flowing over my tongue felt heavenly. "Thank you," I breathed gratefully. Turning my attention back to the conversation, I listened as Dr. P informed us of the decision we needed to make.

"I know at this point you are hoping to stop labor, and that is why we are using the magnesium. I will warn you right up front, though—if this is real labor, we won't be able to stop it with the magnesium. That will only help if the labor is false.

"One of the more common procedures used in a case like

yours is called cervical cerclage, in which we sew the cervix closed in hopes that birth will be delayed until the suture is removed during the ninth month of gestation."

Dr. P paused, and Galen glanced at me before turning back to the doctor. "What are the risks involved in this procedure?" he inquired.

Dr. P's eyes met mine, and I read kindness there. Sensing that he would do everything he could to help us, I felt myself relaxing. "While cerclage is generally a safe procedure, there are several potential complications that may arise during or after surgery.

"There are always the general risks associated with regional or general anesthesia—bleeding and infection. Then there are also the possibilities of premature rupture of the membranes or infection of the amniotic sac." He glanced at me. "C-section could become necessary if you fail to dilate normally. Cervical rupture can also occur if the stitch is not removed before the onset of labor. But as I said before, it is generally safe and has a fairly high success rate." He watched our faces expectantly. "Perhaps you would like some time to think about it?"

"Yes, I think we would," Galen affirmed. "We'll talk it over and let you know how we want to proceed."

"All right, we'll get you another injection of steroids to keep speeding up the infant's lung development. Let me know if you want to pursue further preventive measures. Otherwise we'll just try to keep you comfortable for now and hope for the best."

I felt unsure about the decision that faced us. As I met Galen's eyes, I read the same uncertainty there. "What are you thinking we should do?" I asked.

"I really don't know. It feels like an awfully big decision

to make. Let's pray about it first. Then I think we need to seek some counsel."

By late evening my contractions had grown stronger. My cervix was fully effaced, the baby's head had moved down into the birth canal, and my water bag was bulging. Dr. P thought the baby could come during the night.

It was a long night for both of us as we wrestled with questions, the unknown, and just what decisions we should make. We prayed much, and morning found us weary but grateful that the baby had not yet arrived. Labor had virtually ceased, and we felt hopeful. Still we felt no closer to an answer than we had the night before.

"Esther, Pastor James and Velma are coming up to see us. They'll be here in about an hour," Galen announced as he entered the room after stepping out to make a phone call. "Your dad and mom said they plan to come up sometime this afternoon and bring the girls. Lon and Leona will come down to meet them here and take the girls home for the night." My sister Leona and her husband Lon lived in Lexington, Indiana, which was less than an hour north of Louisville.

"Good," I sighed. "Maybe they'll be able to tell us what we should do."

Galen nodded ruefully. "I certainly hope they can at least give us some advice."

The monitor assured us everything was still well with the baby. My oxygen levels were a bit low, so they put me on oxygen. My movement was severely restricted to try to stop labor. My mouth was dry again, and I sucked despairingly on the ice chips they brought me. It was just enough moisture to tantalize me, but they didn't want to give me more fluids because of the chance of surgery.

"Good morning, Galen, Esther," our minister greeted us. "How are things going?" His kind voice was like a soothing balm in the midst of our turmoil.

His wife Velma stood beside my bed, a reassuring smile on her pleasant face as she asked, "How are you this morning?"

"Oh, I'm all right. It's been a long night. But we're grateful the baby hasn't come yet."

She nodded empathetically.

"Has anything changed since last night?" James inquired.

"Well, we haven't reached a decision yet about whether or not to have a procedure done," Galen replied wearily. "We were wondering if you and Velma might have some advice for us."

They listened quietly as we explained the situation and the option of cervical cerclage. "I've never felt so at a loss as to what to do," Galen confessed. "We've been praying and just don't seem to have any clear sense of direction yet. We don't feel completely right about the procedure, but doing nothing doesn't seem like a good option either."

"Well, I really don't know what to tell you," James said slowly. He paused. "We'll pray with you and trust that the Lord will give you guidance." We bowed our heads and committed the situation into God's hands.

After a half hour of visiting, James turned to Galen. "Velma and I are going to step out for a while. We don't want to wear you out." He smiled at me. "But we'll just be in town here. If you need anything, you can call our cell phone."

"Thanks, James. We really appreciate your coming," Galen said gratefully. "The prayers and support of the church mean a lot right now."

"We're happy to help in any way we can," James assured him.

All through that day we continued to wrestle with our impending decision. Both our sets of parents came to sit with us for a while, and James and Velma returned. No one had any specific advice for us. Even the doctors didn't make a strong recommendation.

By late afternoon, our crucial situation looked completely overwhelming. I was having contractions again, and it made me feel anxious. In one of our moments alone, I told Galen that I felt like throwing up my hands in despair. He took my hand, and we again implored our heavenly Father to show us what to do.

Within the hour our decision was made. We would not pursue cervical cerclage. With our minds made up, a peace settled over our hearts. We knew the Lord had divinely directed our hearts, and we sensed that He was in complete control of our situation.

Lon and Leona arrived toward evening, and by then my contractions had begun to slow with the help of medication. Leona sat down beside me on the bed and our eyes met. In their gentle brown depths I read understanding that can come only from a sister. "We'll keep the girls as long as you need us to." She squeezed my hand, and I smiled gratefully.

"I'm not sure how long this is going to last, but they said something about staying in the hospital on bed rest the last time we discussed things with the doctor." I shook my head in frustration. "I certainly hope I don't have to do that, though. I hate being alone in the hospital, especially at night."

She nodded sympathetically. "Hopefully you won't have to."

Being surrounded by people most of the day had really

helped to pass the time. Now as evening came on and Galen and I were left alone, I thought of bed rest with increasing dread.

"Galen, I just don't think I can do it." My eyes filled with unshed tears. "You know how I hate hospitals at night. I feel like I can't stay here alone for weeks on end. And the girls need me."

"We'll do whatever it takes to save the baby, honey. You'll be okay. Maybe one of your sisters or your mom can come down when I can't be here."

I shook my head. "I don't think I can handle being here without you." My voice broke, and my emotions threatened to overwhelm me. After a night without sleep, two stressful days, and all the uncertainty, I just couldn't take the thought of being left alone without Galen. He understood my feelings and considerately turned the conversation to other subjects.

About 7 p.m., a team from the Kosair Children's Hospital came over to talk to us. Norton Hospital, where we were situated in Labor and Delivery, and Kosair Children's Hospital were connected by a pedway above the street.

Dr. Shultz was the spokesman for the group of three. His close-cropped hair and the firm set of his square jaw added to the professional presentation of the white coat he wore. His sober eyes met mine before he turned to Galen.

"Good evening, Mr. Lengacher. It's a pleasure to meet you." He shook hands with Galen. "Although I wish it were under different circumstances." He glanced at the nurse practitioner who had accompanied him. I noted that, though her face appeared friendly, she wore a concerned expression.

"I assume you are aware that if things continue to progress, you will be faced with the decision of whether or not you want to try to resuscitate." Galen nodded. "The chance of survival for the fetus at this stage of gestation is very slim. In fact, at 22 weeks, the average survival rate is 0 to 5 percent."

We both nodded as he continued. "We do not expect you to try to save the baby's life at this stage. If you simply desire to hold it and let it expire, this might be your wisest option. If you choose to resuscitate, we will do our best, but the odds of a positive outcome are very slim. And . . ."

I glanced at Galen to see how he was receiving this information. His face was calm, but I detected a hint of worry there too.

"Granted the baby does survive the odds of delivery at such a premature stage, you are almost guaranteed that the child will be handicapped for life, more or less severely depending on numerous factors. But the road will be very long and difficult for both the parents and the child."

When they left, I turned to Galen and sighed. I was tired of all the white-coated predictions and grim possibilities, and I was ready for a diversion. "Galen, have you thought any more about choosing a name for our baby?"

"Your mom and dad left the name book here. Why don't you go ahead and look through it for a bit while I step out and call to make some arrangements for the chores."

I relaxed a little as I opened the name book to the girls' names section. Starting at the beginning, I perused through the lists of names and meanings. Suddenly a name jumped out at me: Angelika (an-JEL-i-ka)—"Angelic Messenger."

How fitting, I thought. *Especially if our little one is taken to heaven right away. We'll have another little angel up there.*

When Galen returned some time later, I handed him the book so he could look through it. "I actually had some time to look through it earlier," he told me. "Was there any name that you especially liked?"

"Well, there was one that kind of jumped off the page at me."

"What was it?" he asked with a curious twinkle in his eye.

"Angelika," I said.

A broad grin broke over his face. I raised my eyebrows. "Why the smile?"

"That same name jumped out at me."

"That's great!" I said. "Have you thought about a middle name?"

"I was thinking Rose might sound nice."

"I like that," I agreed. "Angelika Rose. I think it's pretty."

As night descended on the city, things seemed under control and we turned our weary minds to some much-needed sleep.

Miracle in the Night

—Galen

I awoke with a start around 4 a.m. and wondered groggily where I was. As the hospital room came into focus, I saw Esther sitting up in bed. "Galen, I think my water just broke." Her voice was urgent. Suddenly I was wide awake.

"What did you say?" I wasn't quite sure if I had heard her right.

"I'm pretty sure my water broke." There was a hint of fear in her voice.

"Your water broke? I'll call a nurse!" Moving quickly now, I pressed the call button and began praying silently.

"Yes, your membranes have ruptured," the nurse informed us briskly. "We'll get things going as quickly as possible here. I'm going to give you something to speed up labor to make it less stressful for the baby, and then we'll start preparations for delivery right away." My eyes met Esther's, and our hearts united in a silent plea for God's intervention on our behalf.

"Esther, I'm going to call our parents and let them know what's going on. Is that okay?" She nodded, and I stepped out into the hall.

"Hello?" My mom's voice sounded sleepy, and I realized it was still practically the middle of the night.

"Hi, Mom. Galen here. It may not be long until the baby's born."

"All right, Dad and I will head up there right away. We'll be there as soon as we can."

I thanked her, hung up the phone, and punched in Esther's parents' number. "Hello?" another groggy voice answered.

"Hello, Dad, this is Galen." I hastily repeated my message.

He assured me they would come as soon as they could. I took a deep breath and silently acknowledged that God was with us before stepping back into Esther's room.

"The baby feels really low," Esther told me. I held her hand as I sat beside her on the bed.

"Kendra," I announced as a nurse came into view. "Esther says the baby feels really low."

Kendra gave Esther a quick examination. "Yes, it is really low. I'll be back."

The wall clock read 4:19. Outside the hospital room window, the sky was still an inky black.

As Kendra scurried from the room, I turned my attention back to Esther, whose contractions were coming in earnest now. Several minutes passed and Kendra did not return. I glanced at the clock again and wondered where she was. It was 4:26 a.m. "You're doing great," I encouraged as Esther clung to my hand through another contraction.

"I feel like I need to push."

"Okay, go ahead."

With Esther's second push, I caught the whole baby. She fit into the cup of my two hands perfectly, a miniature miracle. Her pitiful arms and legs waved wildly, and she let out miniscule mewing sounds that were hardly audible.

A jolt of adrenalin rushed through me. Still holding her, I rushed to hit the call button with my elbow. "Help, the baby's here!" I yelled.

Almost instantly, a young woman appeared at the door. Her eyes widened in surprise when she saw the baby in my hands. Crossing the room, she grabbed supplies.

Within seconds, several more nurses arrived. Kendra, our labor and delivery nurse, rushed in. Her face was a picture of shock. She cut the cord, took the baby from me, and handed her to the nurse who had first arrived.

Elizabeth, the young woman who had first responded to my call for help, had just completed the hospital's orientation for delivery. Normally she would have been at the nurses' station in the children's hospital at this time of the morning. For some reason, though, she felt she needed to go check supplies in Norton's labor and delivery section this morning.

Just as she was passing outside our room, I called for help. To us she was an angel. As I watched her work diligently over the little life, her large eyes met mine for a fraction of a second, and I saw fear mingled with determination.

The baby responded quickly to resuscitation. The masks were too large, though, and Elizabeth had to make a circle with her fingers and place the bag over them to make it small enough to fit the tiny face.

I glanced over at Esther to see how she was doing. She was surrounded by nurses, and they seemed to have things under control.

At that moment Dr. Stapp walked in. "What are you doing?" she demanded, addressing Elizabeth.

Elizabeth looked up. "I'm resuscitating." Her voice was strained.

"Are you sure they want you to?" Dr. Stapp's brow furrowed disapprovingly.

"I'm pretty sure they do."

"Is the baby doing anything for you?" Dr. Stapp's voice sounded uncertain.

"We're breathing for her, but she's got a heart rate." Elizabeth's words held a question, as if wondering if she should proceed.

Dr. Stapp turned to me. "What do you want us to do, Mr. Lengacher? Do you want us to try to save her?"

"We want you to do everything you can to help her make it," I responded readily. Dr. Stapp nodded and turned back to the baby, preparing to intubate her.

They swaddled her tightly and took her over to Esther. I watched Esther's face as she caught a glimpse of our little girl. My heart constricted. I doubted that our baby would make it. They put her on a warmer for transport to the NICU and trundled into the hall.

Turning to Esther, I noticed the clock on the wall now read 4:45. Everything had happened in just a few short moments, but it felt like it had been hours. I looked down at Esther's flushed face and took her hand. As she raised weary eyes to mine, I saw tears forming in their blue depths.

"She's in God's hands, dear. You've done well." I put my

arm around her and she leaned against me. So much had happened in such a short time, and I could tell she was still in a daze.

"She's so tiny." Her voice broke, and I felt tears coming to my own eyes.

"I know. She's our little angel." Together we cried as we let the last half hour's events soak into our hearts. Secretly, I doubted that we'd ever see our little girl alive again. It felt nonsensical to hope, yet I wrestled internally. *Lord, it feels like we've lost so many children already. I don't want to lose this one too! I can hardly face the thought right now. It just somehow doesn't seem right. We've gone through so much— done all we could. Please, God, could you spare us this one precious little life?*

A short time later my parents arrived. Their faces mirrored care and concern as they greeted us. "The baby's here," I announced without preamble.

"How is she?" Neither registered surprise. This was what they had expected.

"She's . . . tiny." I couldn't think of a whole lot more to say. Mom went over to give Esther a hug, and we all pulled up chairs.

Soon Esther's parents arrived as well. Esther's mom perched on the side of the bed and talked quietly with her for several moments.

"Why don't we pray?" Esther's dad suggested. His weathered face betrayed no feeling, but his voice was deep with emotion. Around Esther's hospital bed, we thanked God for the gift He had granted us, now fighting for survival.

As I listened to the prayers of our godly parents and

mingled my own heart cry with theirs, I sensed God's comforting presence. He was with us, and He would see us through whatever He called us to face.

Esther was exhausted. She dozed for a bit while the rest of us sat around and visited. Twice I inquired at the nurses' station if we could go see the baby. At 8:30 we were finally given the go-ahead, and I took our two mothers back to see her.

As we crossed the pedway to Kosair, I glanced down at the busy street below. That bleak morning, February 15, 2008, looked like any other day, but for us, life would never be the same.

At the double doors of the NICU, we were instructed to scrub our hands. "Three minutes," we were told. I grinned at my mom as the suds washed down the drain. "Makes me feel like a child again."

"Oh, Galen, I never made you scrub this long," she laughed.

After we donned gowns and rubbed in sanitizer, a nurse took my mom and me into the NICU. Only two of us could go back at a time, and Esther's mother had agreed to let my mom go first. As we entered the world of incubators, beeping ventilators, tubes, machinery, and bright lights, I felt intimidated. I caught a glimpse of a baby in an isolette as we passed, and my heartbeat quickened. In just a moment I'd be seeing Angelika!

As we stepped into section F, I peered through the plastic walls of the isolette. She was even smaller than I remembered. Her skin was dark, yet so thin it was nearly translucent. Her tiny ribs protruded sharply from her chest cavity. Her wee nose was just visible from under the light pink band over her eyes. Her whole right foot, except for a row of miniature toes, was encased in a teensy strip of bandage that held an IV in place.

"What does she weigh?" Mom's voice was filled with awe.

"Seventeen ounces," I replied. "She's just eleven inches long."

"Much too little to be ready for the real world." Mom shook her head. "I'm amazed they can even handle babies this size, much less keep them alive."

I nodded. Out of the corner of my eye, I saw a nurse making her way from the back section of the NICU toward us. When she reached us, she said, "I had to come over and see this micro-preemie everyone's been talking about." She smiled and peered into the incubator.

"Oh my, she is tiny, isn't she!" She straightened up and addressed me. "So are they taking care of you? Giving you everything you need?"

I smiled. "Oh, we're doing fine."

"Have they given you a book yet? The one about what to expect with your preemie?" I shook my head. "All right, I'll go get you one." She bustled off and was back shortly.

"Here you are. There's a lot of good information in here. But no one can really predict things. You really just have to take one day at a time when you're dealing with such extreme cases of prematurity."

"Thank you," I said gratefully. "This is a new experience for us, and I think we have a lot to learn."

"You'll adjust," she assured. "And we'll help you along every step of the way."

Later that afternoon, after Esther had rested some more, I took her over to see Angelika. As I pushed her wheelchair across the pedway, we were both silent. I wondered what she would think when she saw our little girl.

As we stood together at the isolette, I watched Esther's face. Her eyes took in the tubes and wires surrounding our baby, and her forehead wrinkled with concern. She stood for a long moment, her eyes tracing the delicate fingers and the tiny chin. At last she looked up and our eyes met. "She's alive, Galen."

I smiled. "I know, and that's a miracle in itself."

I knew my wife was exhausted, so our first private visit with Angelika lasted only a few minutes. "Let's pray over our daughter before we go," I suggested.

She nodded, and together we bowed our heads and prayed blessing and protection over this precious life God had entrusted to us. Whatever we faced in the coming days, we knew that we could depend on His faithfulness through it all.

4 Reality Hits

—Esther

"We'll have to stay somewhere nearby." Galen looked at me uncertainly.

I had just been discharged from the hospital. Angelika's arrival that morning seemed like a distant event as we tried to wade our way through the decisions at hand.

"The Ronald McDonald House is located just down the street from the hospital," a helpful nurse volunteered. "But you'll have to go through a social worker to get in. The first contact is made by the hospital, and then you get a number and wait until a room opens up." With few other options open to us, we immediately began the process of securing a room, hoping and praying we could get in yet that evening.

In the meantime, Lon and Leona arrived with the girls for a short visit. It was so good to see my dear little ones again! I cuddled first Darika and then Alisha. Stroking back her silky blond hair, I kissed Alisha's forehead. "How's my

Alisha today?" I asked, pulling her closer. "I've missed you."

She looked up at me with a sparkle of mischief in her blue eyes. "We had fun," she told me significantly. I looked over at Leona questioningly, and she smiled.

"They've been really good. We're enjoying them a lot."

I felt thankful all over again for a safe place for my little girls to be while we faced our present crisis.

Looking down at Alisha, I asked, "What have you been doing?"

"Valerie played baby with me." Her little face lit up with a smile.

"How fun. Did you know we have a new baby?" I smiled down at her. She searched my face questioningly.

"Where is she, Mama?"

"She's a very little baby—so tiny that she has to be in a special place. She's much smaller than either you or Darika were when you came to us."

"Can I see her?"

"Not now, but hopefully sometime."

"Okay." She seemed content with my answer and scooted across the bed to where Galen sat. Darika crawled up onto my lap, and I glanced across at Galen and smiled wearily. Even though I was tired, it felt so good to be back together as a family.

"So have you decided where you are going to stay while you're here?" Lon questioned.

"We're hoping to get in at the Ronald McDonald House just down the street here," Galen replied. "It's only ten dollars a day, which certainly beats hotel rates."

"What are you thinking about chores?" Lon pursued. "Our boys are happy to stay at your house and help as long as you need them."

"We really appreciate them helping out when I can't be there," Galen replied. "We're still talking about how we're going to do things. I'm not sure how we'll work it all out, but we'll let you know as soon as we can."

"No hurry. I just wanted you to know they're available for as long as you need them," Lon assured him.

"Thanks, Lon. I'm really grateful for their help right now. I'm especially glad that Jared has worked with the chickens before. I can feel at ease, assured that he knows what he's doing."

I listened to the conversation and wondered how things would unfold in the days ahead. Everything was so uncertain. Tracing the angel kiss birthmark on Darika's forehead, I kissed her chubby cheek and brushed my face against her fuzzy head. Holding her close, I savored her soft sweetness. She looked up into my face with trusting blue eyes, and I wondered if I could bear to part with my little ones again. I realized I needed them almost as much as they needed me.

"Well, I suppose we should be going." Lon glanced at his watch and stood up. "We'll keep praying." Leona slipped her arm around my shoulder and I returned her hug as best as I could with Darika still in my arms.

"Thank you so much for taking care of our girls," I said softly. "It means so much to me not to have to worry about their wellbeing."

"That's the way we want it to be," Leona smiled. "It's our pleasure. I know that what you are facing right now isn't easy. Just know we're here to help in any way we can."

Swallowing the lump that had formed in my throat, I kissed Darika one last time and handed her to my sister. "Wave bye-bye to Mama," Leona said. She lifted Darika's little hand and helped her wave goodbye. The lump in my throat returned, and this time tears threatened to follow suit.

Galen took a short walk down the hall to inquire about the Ronald McDonald House again. When he came back, his face had brightened into a smile. "Esther, it looks like there's an opening!" he exulted. "They said the room they have open right now is really small, but that's all we'll need till the girls join us, and that won't be for a little while yet."

"Good." I smiled weakly.

"Are you up to touring our new home?" he asked.

I nodded.

Soon we parked in front of the Ronald McDonald House, an attractive four-story block building with a decorative, castle-style front. Turrets stood on either side of the triple arches that sheltered the bright blue entrance doors.

As we stepped inside, I caught sight of a life-sized statue of Ronald McDonald in his typical yellow and red garb. We went up the open stairway and passed into the foyer beyond, where a smiling, gray-haired woman met us. She held a large set of keys.

"We've been told there's a room for us here." Galen smiled at the woman in his usual friendly manner. "Are you the tour guide?"

"I certainly am." The woman's name tag told us her name was Ann. "Welcome to the Ronald McDonald House. Just follow me and I'll show you around."

As we made our way through the spacious halls and peeked into the model rooms, my heart constricted with longing to go home. Everything seemed so unfamiliar, and the emotional stress of the past few days was beginning to hit me.

She showed us the family-style bathroom and laundry

room we'd be sharing with several other families on our floor and informed us that we were responsible for cleaning our own room. Then she opened the door to a little room and showed us inside. "This is the room we have open." She looked at us expectantly. "Will it suit?"

"It looks good," Galen replied quickly. "Thank you."

"You're welcome. We want you to feel at home, so just let us know if you need anything. Supper is brought in every night by volunteers and served down in the main cafeteria on the first floor. Do you have any questions?"

Galen glanced at me before answering. "I don't think so. Thank you, Ann. We really appreciate your taking the time to show us around and make us feel at home."

"You're certainly welcome. Here's your key, and I wish you the best of luck." Then she was gone, and we were alone.

I sank wearily onto the bed and looked up at Galen in mute appeal.

"It's been a long day, hasn't it?" He sat down beside me and slipped his arm around my shoulders. "We should be able to rest easier here than we did in the hospital, though. At least we have privacy." I nodded, grateful in spite of my exhaustion.

"Why don't you stay here and rest while I go get our things?" Galen suggested. "I'll try to find something for us to eat, and then we can snooze." Glad to get off my feet, I kicked off my shoes and sank back onto the soft whiteness of the full-sized bed. My whole body ached, and I longed to rest, but my emotions kicked in and my mind replayed the details of the last few days. Silent tears coursed down my cheeks as I waited.

After a little while, Galen returned. He set our bags near the door and sat on the edge of the bed. "How does pizza sound?"

I sat up. "Truthfully, I don't really care what we eat."

He nodded understandingly. "It's been a tremendously stressful few days, hasn't it? I hope you can get some rest tonight."

He opened the carry-out box of pizza, still hot, and we bowed our heads, thanking God for the food and asking Him to care for Angelika. I thought of the helpless, tiny form lying under bright lights somewhere in that great big hospital, and tears sprang to my eyes. I wondered how much longer she would hold on.

Galen clasped my hand as he continued, "And, Lord, I pray especially for Esther tonight. Please give her rest. Help her to heal quickly and fully. In Jesus' name, Amen."

Tears were streaming down my cheeks when he looked up. The pent-up stress of the past days, the separation from our girls, and the looming uncertainty of everything crashed in on me as reality truly hit. Silently Galen wrapped his arm around me. I leaned against him and sobbed.

When the storm of tears subsided, I felt slightly better. Yet silent tears continued to slide down my cheeks as I slowly ate a piece of the pizza that had grown cold.

That night I couldn't feel God's nearness. The world looked black. I fell asleep, still crying.

5 His Hands and Feet

—*Esther*

The next day we went over to visit Angelika as soon as we could. I quickly tired of standing, so I went out to the waiting room, leaving Galen to spend some time alone with his newest daughter.

The clock on the wall read 11:30 a.m. I flipped restlessly through the *Taste of Home* magazine on the small table beside me, wondering how many hours in the days ahead I would spend here in this drab little waiting room. It wasn't the most inviting place in the world, especially not when my head was aching with exhaustion and emotional fatigue. In spite of the comfortable bed in the Ronald McDonald House, I had slept restlessly. My body still needed a lot of good rest. Yet I knew I didn't want to be anywhere but here, close to our baby.

"Hello, Esther. How are you?" I glanced up as a familiar voice greeted me. Geneva Peachy's smiling face broke into my world like a ray of bright sunshine. Her husband Paul walked in behind her, carrying a large cooler.

"We just thought we'd come up and see how you folks are getting along," Paul grinned, setting his burden down near the door. I was surprised and delighted to see these good friends of ours from church.

"It's so good to see familiar faces!" I said.

Geneva and I exchanged a warm hug, and I invited them to sit down. "Galen's back with the baby right now," I explained. "I'll go get him."

When Galen entered the waiting room, Paul's face broadened into a grin. "Hello, brother. How's it going? We've been praying a lot ever since the prayer chain went around. When we heard the baby had arrived, we thought you might be a bit lonely up here."

Paul and Geneva knew what it was like to watch over a baby in the NICU. Their little girl had spent several weeks in the hospital, having been born with a heart condition. My heart warmed with gratitude for their faithful, thoughtful friendship.

"It sure means a lot," Galen responded heartily. "Would you like to see Angelika?"

They nodded, and Galen glanced over at me. "I'll take Paul and then you can take Geneva. Is that all right?" I nodded and the two men disappeared.

"So how are you feeling, Esther? Have you been able to get any rest?" Geneva's kind brown eyes searched my face. "I know it can't be easy right now."

I told her what the last few days had been like and how exhausted I was. Geneva nodded in understanding. Her emotional support strengthened my sagging spirits.

When it was our turn to see Angelika, Geneva stood in

front of the isolette, her eyes wide with amazement. "It's astounding that such a tiny human is actually alive," she murmured.

"I know," I agreed, realizing again just how frail my baby looked.

Before they left, Paul nodded toward the cooler by the door. "That cooler has some food we thought you might be able to use in the next week or so. We'll be praying blessings on you."

Paul and Geneva were like angels of encouragement to me. Grateful tears filled my eyes as I watched them walk out the door. I glanced over at Galen and read the same feeling in his face.

Rrrinngg.

"Hello." Galen looked over at me with a knowing grin. We had barely returned to our room in the Ronald McDonald House before the phone started to ring. This was the third call in fifteen minutes. I watched his face curiously, wondering who it was this time.

"Hi, Don. Yeah, things are going well. We're just taking it one hour at a time. All right, sounds good! We'll see you then."

"Are Don and Lorene coming?" I asked, surprised. My older sister and her husband lived in Antrim, Ohio. Making the trip down to us would take quite a sacrifice of their time.

"Yup, they're coming tomorrow."

"That's so good of them. I'll be glad not to be alone over Sunday," I mused.

"The way things are looking right now, I don't think we're going to have a chance to get lonely," Galen noted. "With four couples visiting today and more already lined up for tomorrow, it looks like we'll be in good shape. And the way this phone's been ringing this evening—" His words were cut short by another insistent ring.

This time it was our minister, James. He and his wife wanted to come up the next day as well. "We could have our own little service up here," Galen chuckled. "Oh, I forgot to tell you, Esther. Your brother Leroy called this morning and said they hope to come sometime tomorrow too."

Later that evening, Galen went over to see Angelika one last time before bedtime. When he returned, he informed me that Icy, a Christian nurse we knew, was going to care for Angelika that night.

We had instantly sensed there was something special about Icy, who was originally from India. Her gentle spirit emanated peace, and we soon discovered that she was a believer. I sighed gratefully. It meant so much to know that our baby was in good hands. "God is really looking out for us, isn't He?"

"He sure is," Galen agreed. "I couldn't wish for better nurses than Angelika's had so far."

"You know, Galen, it felt as though God was so far away last night. But today He sent so many of His people to minister to our needs. I feel as if He's been especially close today."

"His people have certainly been Christ's hands and feet to us. I hope we can be the same to those around us here. And I anticipate that, with all the hurting people in a hospital, we'll get plenty of opportunities. Did I mention the couple

I met in the hall last night on my way up here?"

"No, I don't think you did."

"They have a preemie in the NICU right now too, and they're staying here at the Ronald McDonald House as well. If I remember right, their names are Ben and Liz Turner. They seemed like the kind of folks who would make good friends."

At the moment I didn't know if I was too eager to make new friends. The crisis we were facing took enough emotional effort without the added work of forming new relationships, but I appreciated my social husband's desire to reach out to others.

Sunday dawned clear and cold, but the sun shone brightly as we made our way over to the hospital. I felt a bit more rested than I had the day before and I anticipated seeing my brothers and sister, who planned to visit that morning.

The smell of disinfectant and the warmth of the indoors washed over us as we stepped off the elevators and made our way toward the NICU. Together we scrubbed and entered Section F.

Standing on either side of the isolette, we watched Angelika as she lay under a blue light, asleep. Her chest rose and fell, making her toothpick-like ribs stick out painfully. We couldn't see much of her body due to all the tubes, wires, and gauze that covered her. My throat constricted and tears pricked my eyelids. Galen's eyes met mine across the top of the isolette, and he smiled.

"The nurses say she seems to be doing amazingly well," he reassured me.

Just then a nurse approached us. "You can talk to her

if you like," she said, smiling. "Soft words soothe babies." Then she turned away to another one of her charges.

"Angelika, you are very precious to us, little one." Galen's voice was low and crooning. "We love you. Keep up the good fight. You can do it. You're a strong little girl."

After we ended our morning visit with Angelika, we walked back out to the waiting room again. Galen noticed the couple he had mentioned to me the night before, and he greeted them warmly. "Ben, Liz. This is my wife Esther. I was hoping she'd get a chance to meet you folks soon."

Ben grinned jovially. "Glad to meet you." He shook my hand warmly. Liz looked like a friendly, gracious woman, and I felt instantly drawn to her. We began to share about our families, our babies, and hospital life in general. My hesitancy at making new friends melted away as I found common ground with these people.

As soon as Ben and Liz left, my sister Lorene and her family arrived. They all found seats in the waiting room and we began to visit. Not much later, my brothers Leroy and James and their wives joined us.

The morning flew by as we talked, and soon it was time for lunch. Back at the Ronald McDonald House, we enjoyed the ample lunch my sister and in-laws had brought. "So do you have more company coming tonight?" Leroy inquired, looking up from his piece of pie.

"Several families from our church are coming, including Pastor James and Velma," Galen replied, refilling his glass with water.

"Mom and Dad are coming up too," I added. "We've been so blessed by all our visitors in the last few days."

After my family's departure, Galen and I had several hours to relax before our next round of company arrived that evening.

As they arrived, they all took turns seeing Angelika, oohing and aahing about her miniature perfection. When we were all gathered back in the waiting room, James inquired if we'd like to have a small service while they were there.

"I was hoping we could," Galen replied. "We can cross the pedway and use the chapel over at Norton Hospital, if you like."

Quietly we filed into the dimly lit chapel. Dark blue carpet covered the floor, matching the seats on the wooden-backed chairs. A small pulpit and an ornately carved wooden table stood at the front of the chapel beneath a wooden cross mounted on the wall. Serenity filled our souls as we found seats and waited for James to begin the service.

"Let's open with a word of prayer," James suggested. Reverently, he prayed for God's presence with us as we came to worship. "Thank you that you are present wherever two or three are gathered in your name." His words stirred my heart with gratitude as I thought of the special people surrounding us with their support and prayers.

Thank you, God, my heart echoed.

"I guess I don't have any notes tonight," James announced. "We'll trust the Lord to lead the service as He sees fit. Let's start by looking at Psalm 46 together." As his gentle voice spoke the powerful words, I was struck by how fitting they were for our situation.

"'God is our refuge and strength, a very present help in trouble.'" How true this had been for us through all the ups and downs of this past week. He had been there to help us each step of the way.

"'Therefore will not we fear,'" James read. "'Though the earth be removed, and though the mountains be carried into the midst of the sea.'" Surely He would be trustworthy through whatever we were called to face in the coming days, even if our world was shaken.

In the chapel's stillness, I pondered the words, "Be still and know that I am God: I will be exalted among the heathen . . ." Perhaps that was why we were here—so that His name would be lifted up and glorified. I felt strength seep into my soul as the comforting promise of His presence and power rested like balm on my weary, questioning heart.

Later as we stood around before they left, each of the men prayed for us in turn. Tears came at the thought of them leaving. Everything still seemed so overwhelming. I broke down and cried silently. Galen slipped an arm around my shoulders in support.

Looking up after the last "Amen," one of the men turned to us. "Make sure you get out from time to time. It's the best thing you can do to maintain your sanity."

"That's for sure," his wife assented. "Even just a quick trip into town can do wonders to refresh you."

At that moment, the advice made little sense to me. It wouldn't feel right to do something fun when our helpless daughter lay alone in the hospital. Still, God would be with her even when we were not.

6 It Can't Be Done!

—*Galen*

"I'm wondering if you could give me a run-down of what our bill is so far," I inquired at the desk.

"I certainly can. And what's your name?" The lady smiled up at me.

"Galen Lengacher." After checking on Esther's delivery bill at Norton Hospital, I was now checking Angelika's bill at Kosair Children's Hospital. Forrest Mast, the man in charge of medical aid at our church, had wanted to meet with me to discuss the financial aspects of our situation. I wanted to gather all the figures I could before he came.

"Okay, here's your bill for the five days you've been here." She laid a printed sheet of figures in front of me. "These are all the individual costs. And here's your total." The bold, black figure at the bottom of the page jumped out at me— **$80,000.**

I drew a deep breath. "So when does this need to be

paid?" I asked.

"You don't have to pay the bill until after discharge. And if you pay it within thirty days of discharge, you will receive an 80-percent discount."

I nodded. "All right. And when we're ready to discuss this, do I come back here with my questions?"

"Yes, all your billing needs can be handled right here."

"Thank you," I said, my mind whirling. *Angelika's bill is enormous compared to Esther's. Just think what this bill could be by the end of the hospital stay!* But I tried not to worry. I knew God would provide all we needed, no matter how big the bill was.

When Forrest arrived a short time later, I took him up to see Angelika. "How's it going for you folks?" he asked as we scrubbed. "We've been praying a lot for you."

"We certainly appreciate all your prayers," I replied. "We're just taking it a day at a time right now and trusting that God will work out whatever He feels is best."

Forrest followed me into the NICU and back to section F. Looking down at Angelika, his eyebrows lifted in an expression of wonder. "She looks so fragile. It's incredible." He shook his head in amazement and held a thick, work-roughened finger against the side of the isolette. "She'd almost fit into the palm of my hand."

I smiled. "We took pictures of her with a pen and a five-dollar bill yesterday. When she scrunches up her legs, she's not much bigger than the bill."

Back in the waiting room we sat down to talk business.

"So you got Esther's bill from Norton Hospital?"

"Right, and they said we can get an 80-percent discount on that one if we pay it within thirty days of when Esther was discharged. On the hospital's bill, that is. The doctors' bills are separate, and a man from the billing department called me about that yesterday. He said we need to talk to him in his office."

"And what about Angelika's bill?"

"I talked with the lady in the billing department of Kosair Children's Hospital this morning and got a printout of our bill so far." I handed him the sheet of paper and watched as he glanced over the figures.

"That's a big bill, isn't it?" He turned to me with a grin, and I nodded with a wry smile. "So our first step is probably to go over and talk to the man in the billing department about paying the doctors, right?"

"Yes. His office is just across the street on the eleventh floor of one of these high-rise buildings." We got up and walked toward the elevator.

As we entered the drab office, a tall figure behind the desk rose to greet us. "Hello, have a seat," he invited. He motioned to two chairs in front of his desk. "I'm André," he introduced himself. We told him our names and sat down.

"So, you are here to discuss billing business. How do you plan to pay for this?" André questioned.

I looked over at Forrest, who replied, "Normally we handle this as a church. We believe it's right to pay our bills."

André gave an incredulous chuckle. "Are you aware of how large this bill is going to be?"

We both shook our heads.

"We're not talking about a hundred thousand here—we're talking a million, and possibly several million, when things are all said and done."

He paused, letting his words take effect. Continuing,

he said, "This isn't just a one-time case, either. It's the type of case that is going to require long-term follow-up care, even after you leave the hospital. The government has aid available specifically for situations like yours."

He looked at us expectantly, but we both shook our heads. "We don't want to take government aid," I said decidedly, and Forrest nodded. I added, "We believe that if God wants Angelika to live, He will provide the means to pay for the bills involved."

André shook his head. "You're not going to be able to handle this as a community, I can tell you that right now. You're going to have to apply for assistance." He seemed convinced that we were considering the impossible. And it certainly looked impossible, even to us, unless God intervened miraculously. But now was the time to put our faith into practice.

"When do you need the first payment?" Forrest inquired. We went on to discuss discounts, billing frequency, and other details. When we were nearly done, André again turned the subject back to how we were going to pay for the bill.

"If you are unable to pay this bill, the hospital cannot refuse you care while you are here. But after you leave, if you need further care and return to the hospital without having covered your bills, they are authorized to turn you away. Are you aware what this might imply?" His dark eyes searched my face, and I waited silently. "If the state hears about it, you could be charged with neglect and the child might be taken from you."

I felt trepidation at his words, yet I knew that God was able to provide for our needs.

"I'm aware that there could be trouble if we do not pay the bill. But we are planning to pay," I concluded.

"It's impossible." He shook his head disbelievingly. "You go home and discuss this as a church and decide what you are going to do, and then we'll talk some more. Remember that there is financial aid available."

"Thank you, André. We'll be in touch about this." Forrest rose and held out his hand.

"All right. Thank you for your time," André replied. He remained cordial, though he obviously believed our faith to be utterly unreasonable.

As we left, I glanced out the office windows to the vast city below us. I wondered how God would take us through our own complex city of decisions and challenges.

"Well, he was certain this couldn't be handled through self-pay." I pushed the large red button, and we entered the elevator.

"Yes, he was," Forrest agreed. "And I have to admit, I've never faced something quite this big before, and it's faith-stretching to consider just how we're going to handle the expenses."

I nodded. "The other day Esther and I agreed that we would be willing to pay on this bill for the rest of our lives if Angelika will just be okay."

"I suppose when you look at it from that perspective, the financial part hardly matters," Forrest agreed. "We'll just have to trust God to provide. I'll bring it up at the next brothers' meeting and see if I can get some wheels turning."

"We so appreciate your support and the support of the church during this time," I told him.

"Well, it's all about God and His glory. I can't see what plans He has in this right now. But that's when our faith is put into action." Forrest and I left the building and parted ways. In spite of the questions I had, I trusted that God was able to meet all our needs.

7 The Peace Speaker

—Galen

The following Thursday, February 21, my phone rang just as we finished cleaning our room at the Ronald McDonald House.

"Hello? . . . Oh, no! We'll be right over." Flipping my phone shut, I said to Esther, "That was the hospital. They want us to come over right away." With a sense of foreboding, we grabbed our coats and headed for the elevator.

Things had been going exceptionally well for Angelika that first week. Our hopes were high, and we had begun to feel as though this might be much easier than we had anticipated. They had even begun moving the settings down on the vent, since Angelika needed less oxygen. We thought she might just sail right through the possible dangers in her further development. But the phone call we had just received threatened to dash our cherished hopes.

We arrived at the hospital moments later. Breathing silent

prayers, we hurried up to the NICU. We were met just outside the NICU by Dr. Robinson. I could tell by the look on her face that things were not good.

"They called you to come up?" It was more of a statement than a question. We nodded. "I'm sorry, but things aren't looking good for Angelika right now." Her eyes met ours sympathetically. "She's been bloating all afternoon, and we found she has a perforated bowel." She shook her head. The look on her face made my stomach sink. "She was doing so well. It's such a shame."

"What is the prognosis?" I asked, trying to wrap my mind around the news we had just received. I could tell by Dr. Robinson's sagging expression that she thought it was all over for Angelika. And I had been told that Dr. Robinson never gave up.

"Well, they'll need to insert a Penrose drain right away. We can't do surgery, because she's too small, but if we don't do something, the condition is fatal. The resident doctor on the surgery team will be over shortly to give you an opinion and talk things over with you."

She turned to go. Esther and I stepped out into the hall. "I guess I'll call the prayer hotlines right away," I said. Besides our own church's hotline, we felt free to call on several other churches of which our close relatives were members. I dialed our minister's number and waited. Glancing over at Esther, I noted the tension on her face. Her eyes filled with unshed tears as she looked away, and I knew this news was even harder on her than it was on me.

James assured me they would put it on the hotline right away. I thanked him and called two other prayer hotlines while we waited for the resident doctor to arrive. When I hung up from the last call, I turned to Esther. "Let's ask if we can go in and see Angelika while we wait."

The nurse assured us that would be fine. We hurried in. Angelika's tummy was distended due to the bloating, and she was running a fever. Questions swarmed through my mind as I tried to sort everything out. Reaching through the holes in the isolette, I touched her hand with my forefinger.

"Esther, let's pray for her," I said. Standing together beside our baby's sickbed, we joined hands and hearts as we cried for help from our heavenly Father, asking Him to heal Angelika and to give wisdom to the doctors. We released our little girl and gave her back to God.

The resident doctor was a brilliant Asian who obviously knew what he was about. Carefully he explained to us what our options were and what we were facing.

"A perforated bowel is a medical emergency that requires surgery. If left untreated, the usual result is blood infection. It can cause almost immediate death."

His eyes didn't leave our faces as he talked. "Due to the size of the patient, we will not be able to perform the necessary surgery immediately. An infant has to be two pounds or more and be in stable condition before we can proceed. Thus the only real alternative open to us is to use local anesthesia and install a Penrose drain. This is a soft rubber tube placed in a wound area to prevent the buildup of fluid and to drain away any fluid that forms. The surgeon then pulls it out just a little bit each day in the hopes that eventually a natural fistula, or drain, will form and take the place of the Penrose drain."

He paused and I asked him, "What is the success rate of the Penrose drain in this sort of case?"

"Well, we'd like to think it's going to do the trick for you, but of course there aren't any guarantees. But," he hastened on as if to assure us, "two thirds of the cases survive, and in one third of these cases no further surgery is necessary; the problem repairs itself. In the other third of these surviving cases, the Penrose drain keeps the problem under control until further surgery is possible. In a third of the cases, the patient doesn't survive."

"And this is our only course of action available?" I asked hesitantly. He replied in the affirmative. It seemed our path had been defined for us. As I searched my wife's face, I knew Esther agreed with me. I turned to the doctor and said, "Do all you can for her."

"Very good. She's in good hands and we'll hope for the best." He shook hands with us and turned to go.

"Where will the procedure be done?" I asked.

"Right here in the NICU," he replied.

I reached out and took Esther's hand as the doctor disappeared around the corner. "How are you doing, dear?"

"You know what? I'm amazingly at peace," she replied. "I was feeling so uptight about all of this, but as soon as you called the prayer chain, I had almost instant peace."

"I'm glad," I smiled. "God really is right here with us. I feel at peace too. Let's just keep trusting Him. I know He has this all under control."

It was a long evening. Esther and I prayed silently as we waited during the procedure.

Around 10:00, the surgeon came to talk to us.

"Good evening, folks." Dr. Foley's voice, though weary, was kind. "Angelika came through all right. She's in critical condition, but we'll hope for the best."

"How long will it be before we know if it was successful?" I asked.

"A few days will tell us a lot. Of course, it varies with each individual case. She's on antibiotics for the infection."

"And you feel like we've done everything we could for her?"

"Yes, we've done everything we can do, medically speaking. Now we'll just have to keep a close eye on her and wait for the outcome."

"Could we see her yet tonight?" I asked.

He told us we could, so we headed for the NICU. As we looked down at Angelika in her highly regulated world of plastic walls, beeping monitors, tubes, and needles, the peace we had felt all evening prevailed. Her eyes were tightly shut, and the ventilator was doing most of the work of breathing for her. On the left side of her groin, covered by a wee piece of gauze, was the one-inch plastic drain that we hoped would save her life. We were fully aware, however, that God was the giver of life. We knew we could trust Him, whatever He chose to do.

"It will be midnight by the time we get back to the Ronald McDonald House." I turned to Esther, and she nodded wearily. Though we were loath to leave our baby, we knew she was in good hands, and we needed sleep to face whatever lay ahead. "We love you, Angelika," Esther whispered huskily before we left.

In the days that followed, Angelika progressed well and was soon in stable condition. As she continued to improve, we began to breathe easier again. Yet the constant, underlying anxiety in our hearts forced us to cling to God's grace daily.

Toward the end of our second week in the hospital, I made arrangements to go home one morning and chore. I planned to leave by 4:00 if possible. I wanted to get back that same morning so Esther wouldn't have to be alone too long.

As I drove toward home through the predawn darkness, my mind churned with all that had taken place in the last two weeks. I felt weighed down with the many responsibilities I was leaving to others back at the house and farm, along with all the unknowns and decisions that stretched away into the future.

Music played softly in the background. It was a tape we had listened to dozens of times before. But as another song started, the words suddenly caught my attention.

> It was such a lovely day,
> and the sun was shining bright;
> A gentle breeze was blowing my way,
> not a storm cloud in sight;
> Then suddenly, without warning,
> a storm surrounded my life—

That sounds familiar, I thought, my mind now fully engaged. The verse continued.

> But even in the storm,
> I can feel the calm,
> and here's the reason why:
> I know the Peace Speaker—
> I know Him by name;
> I know the Peace Speaker—
> He controls the wind and waves;

> When He says, "Peace, be still,"
> they have to obey;
> I'm glad I know the Peace Speaker—
> yes, I know Him by name.

Tears started to my eyes as I listened. "God, it's like you've sent this just for me," I said out loud.

> There's never been another man
> with the power of this Friend;
> By simply saying, "Peace, be still,"
> He can calm the strongest wind;
> That's why I never worry
> when storm clouds come my way—
> I know that He is near to drive away
> my fear, and I can smile and say . . .*
>
> —Geron Davis

Through tears, I glanced up at the star-speckled sky outside my window. "Thank you, God. This is just what I needed right now. Thank you for the reminder that you are our peace, even in the midst of our present storm."

I sensed His presence in a special way in those moments. As I thought about how the God of the universe personally cared for our needs, my cares slipped away. What an opportunity God had given us by placing this child in our care right now. We would be able to testify to the power and faithfulness of God, whatever the outcome. Many were praying, and God had been so faithful to meet our needs even in little ways. That He cared enough to show His power and presence in our lives made me feel small but incredibly loved.

For the rest of the drive, I listened to the remaining songs on the cassette. As daylight began to lighten the sky, I turned in the lane and headed for the barns.

Stepping out of the van, I was greeted with a rush of chilly morning air and the familiar smell of the chicken farm. With renewed joy, I broke into song, echoing the praise that now rang in my heart. "I'm glad I know the Peace Speaker—yes, I know Him by name."

8 A Big God

—Galen

Esther stood beside me, her face drawn with concern. It was Friday, February 29. The doctor had asked to meet with us for consultation about a new issue Angelika was facing. They had noticed swelling in the ventricles of her brain, and they informed us that our baby had hydrocephalus, a fairly typical condition in premature babies, but also potentially dangerous or even fatal.

As I listened now to the prognosis and treatment options, I prayed silently for wisdom and strength. Despite the fact that we had already faced crises with Angelika and had been warned to expect them, I still didn't feel entirely prepared to meet this new development.

"Hydrocephalus, a condition also known as 'water on the brain,' is an abnormal buildup of cerebrospinal fluid, also known as CSF. This fluid builds up in the ventricles, which are the fluid-filled spaces in the center of the brain. Under normal conditions, CSF is produced in the ventricles and then circulates down the spinal cord and back up over the surface of the brain. There it is absorbed by the blood vessels. Hydrocephalus occurs when fluid is being produced faster than it can be absorbed. As CSF builds up, it causes the ventricles to swell and pressure builds inside the brain." The doctor paused, making sure we understood the explanation.

"Hydrocephalus is sometimes present at birth or, as is the case with Angelika, it can develop after birth. This is known as acquired hydrocephalus."

"What causes it?" I wondered.

"Well, there are several causes for acquired hydrocephalus. These include bleeding in the ventricles, meningitis, head trauma, or development of a tumor or cyst. The most common cause of this condition in premature babies is bleeding in the ventricles. When the blood clots, it either blocks the flow of CSF or reduces the brain's ability to reabsorb it, causing the development of hydrocephalus."

I nodded. "Is that the cause of Angelika's condition?"

"More than likely, although we don't know for sure. We've scheduled a CT scan to further assess just what is causing the swelling. We'll do daily X-rays as well to keep tabs on it."

"How is hydrocephalus treated?" I questioned.

"Good question, Mr. Lengacher. Though there is a possibility that the swelling will go down on its own, there is also a good chance that further measures will need to be taken to get the swelling under control."

Esther slipped her hand into mine as the doctor went on to explain our options.

"If the excess CSF does not begin to drain on its own, it is vital that we drain it to prevent the buildup of pressure that can cause damage to the brain. Sometimes when we're dealing with cases like this in the NICU, we can temporarily drain the excess fluid with periodic spinal taps. In premature babies, this often relieves the pressure in the brain while allowing the baby time to grow. Occasionally the obstruction will clear up on its own. Most often, though, the baby will eventually need a more permanent solution. In this case we would surgically place a shunt to drain away the excess fluid from the ventricles to the abdominal cavity, where the CSF is then absorbed into the bloodstream."

I couldn't help asking, "When a shunt is placed, what are the possible complications?" I could see my question mirrored in Esther's eyes, now clouded with worry.

"Well, I wish I could tell you that there is no risk. But, of course, with any surgical procedure there are risks. The outcome depends heavily on the cause of the hydrocephalus as well. Many children with shunts go on to live active, healthy lives with normal intelligence levels. Other children, however, will face issues with motor skills. It can also cause difficulties with vision. The most common complications are learning disabilities. Less common effects could include seizures and sensitivity to noise and bright lights.

"The potential complications of the shunt itself include infection in the brain or the shunt, blood clots or bleeding on the brain, brain swelling, seizures, and damage to brain tissue. There is also the possibility that the shunt may stop working, in which case the fluid will begin to build up on the brain again. However, the risk of infection is relatively low. Statistically, 3 to 12 percent of patients develop a shunt infection. Most of these infections occur within the first three months after surgery, with preemies and other small infants being the most at risk.

"Though I can't give you a guarantee, most often shunt placement is relatively successful in solving hydrocephalus symptoms, and the outcome varies according to the situation and the cause of the condition. Any other questions?"

I pondered a moment. "Is immediate treatment necessary?" Despite the fact that the shunt was perhaps our only option, I didn't like the sound of it.

"It's not mandatory. As I mentioned before, we'll keep a close eye on her. If the swelling increases at all, I feel it would be necessary to act quickly to ensure a positive outcome."

"All right. If we need to go ahead with the shunt, we will, but we'll hope we won't have to," I agreed.

The doctor smiled and stood up. "We'll hope for the best. Thank you for your time."

He shook hands genially and disappeared through the doorway, leaving Esther and me alone.

As I turned to Esther, I saw tears in her eyes. I slipped my arm around her shoulders and we sat in silence for several moments. "Let's pray." It seemed the only thing to do at such a moment. Together we took our burdened hearts to our heavenly Father, asking for the wisdom and comfort that only He could give.

"I'm going to call the prayer chains right away," I said as Esther raised her head.

"All right," she agreed. "We need people's prayers right now. God has done miracles for Angelika before through their prayers."

"And He can do it again if He thinks it's best. We'll just keep trusting Him." I squeezed her hand as I got up to make the phone calls.

Later that night, Esther and I talked about the events of the afternoon. Esther hated the possibility of the shunt. "Galen, I'm just so scared that the swelling won't go down and they'll have to do the procedure."

"I know, I don't like the idea either. But the doctor said many children go on to live normal lives after they have a shunt put in."

"I'm not so sure, though." Esther looked down at her hands. "This probably sounds silly, but when they said that we'd have to be careful that she didn't hit her head, I had to wonder how I would ever manage that in a normal household. I can just picture her having to walk around with a helmet on her head."

I felt the corners of my mouth turning up slightly. "Right, that would never work. But we can't borrow from the future, honey. Only God knows what will happen tomorrow. Just as we trusted Him for today, we need to trust Him with our future. Did I tell you that I met up with Dr. P in the hall today?"

"No, did he say anything to you?"

"Yes, and I was surprised. He looked me in the eye and said, 'Galen, there is a God.' We didn't talk because he was on his way somewhere, but I knew he was talking about Angelika's survival and progress. It was a good reminder that God allows all these things for a purpose."

"Wow," Esther breathed. "It's so good to see evidence of faith in the hospital."

Before dropping off to sleep, we prayed that God would work in a way that would bring Him the most glory. We tried to set aside our selfish desires and fears, and simply commit ourselves into His hands.

Though we had been hoping to attend our church back

home that Sunday, we decided to stick around the hospital due to Angelika's condition. We spent much time in prayer, adjusting our minds and hearts to the possibilities before us. As in every previous crisis, we felt God's peace through His Spirit and the prayers of His people.

On Sunday afternoon they took Angelika down to another floor for a CT scan. The results showed that, though the swelling had not gone down, her condition had not worsened. We breathed a bit easier when we heard the news.

The doctor told us they thought a small bleed had caused the condition. "Things don't look nearly as bad as they could have. You're lucky," he said meaningfully. "We'll keep on watching her closely for a while."

On Monday we were thrilled to hear that the swelling was slowly lessening as the fluid drained. We kept praying. By Wednesday morning the doctor informed us that, though it would take a little while to heal, the present crisis was past. If the swelling didn't return, they wouldn't have to put in the shunt.

The smile on Esther's face mirrored my own. How our hearts rejoiced in the faithfulness and healing power God had chosen to display in Angelika! Later, looking down into her tiny face, I whispered. "We serve a big God, Angelika. And He loves you!"

Deep down I knew that no matter what God allowed to happen, this was still true. Circumstances couldn't change His love for us. But I couldn't help feeling especially loved that night as I rejoiced in the miracle God had performed for us. Cupping my hands over Angelika, I quietly hummed a hymn of thanks.

9 Settling In

—*Esther*

As we left the city behind, I leaned back in my seat and closed my eyes. I could just picture our reunion already. It would feel so good to have my girls in my arms again!

We had visited them at Lon's house a few times in the past three weeks. I always looked forward to these trips, but parting again was excruciating. I hoped that soon I would be strong enough for them to come join us at the Ronald McDonald House, but I just wasn't quite ready yet. I willed myself to focus on the positive and smiled as I pictured the excited sparkle in Alisha's blue eyes and the merry grin on Darika's cherub face.

"Mama is here! Mama is here!" Alisha ran and threw her arms around my legs.

"How are you, Alisha?" I asked, bending down to kiss her upturned face. Behind her came my niece, holding Darika. Alisha ran to her daddy next, and I reached down to take

Darika. "How's my baby?" I brushed my cheek against her soft face and hugged her tightly, relishing her solid, wiggling goodness.

Just before we left, it was time for Darika's bottle. I sat in a rocking chair in the corner of the living room and cuddled her close as she sucked hungrily. I gazed into her eyes, those blue depths so unquestioningly trustful. I savored the moment, realizing anew just how lost I really felt without my little girls to care for. As Darika's eyes closed drowsily, I felt tears come to my eyes.

How could I bear to leave my babies behind one more time? The tears flowed thick and fast now, raining silently down my cheeks and falling on Darika's soft pink blanket. I took her chubby little hand in mine and stroked it gently. Her fingers closed in a firm grip around mine, as if she wanted to ensure that I wouldn't leave her. "Oh, sweet little baby! Mama doesn't want to go."

I watched as the last drops of milk drained from the bottle. Her breathing slowed, and her fingers loosened as she relaxed into sleep. Wiping my tears, I rose to lay her down. Planting a last kiss on her forehead, I tiptoed away.

As we drove back toward the city, my heart ached. Galen broke the silence. "It wasn't easy to say goodbye, was it?"

I shook my head. "I don't think I can do it much longer. Do you think we can bring them here to stay with us soon?"

"Are you feeling strong enough for that now? It's going to mean a lot of extra caregiving, but I'm ready whenever you are."

"I think I could handle it. I'm ready to try."

"All right, we'll pick them up early next week. How does that sound?" He grinned at me and reached out to take my hand.

"Sounds good." I leaned back wearily. "I just want us to be a family again."

We were given a larger room at the Ronald McDonald House, and by Monday morning we were ready for the girls to join us. Lon and Leona brought them down Monday evening to save us the trip. As we all knelt for prayer before going to bed, we thanked the Lord for bringing our family back together again.

Despite a bit of apprehension as to how that first night would go, both girls slept quite well. When I woke up late the next morning to sunshine streaming in our window, I lay still and savored the sight of the two relaxed forms in the bed next to ours. It just felt so right to have them with us again.

Galen had gone over early to spend time with Angelika, as he often did in the mornings. The sounds of city bustle below us were in full swing. I checked the time and saw it was 9:00. *The girls must be worn out to be sleeping so late,* I thought as I swung my bare feet over the edge of the bed. *Maybe I'll have time to get ready for the day before they wake up.*

When Galen got back, we all ate a late breakfast of cold cereal in the Ronald McDonald House dining room. "Shall we all go over to the hospital when we're done here so you can spend time with Angelika?" Galen asked.

I shoveled another spoonful of Cheerios into Darika's mouth before answering. "Could we just let the girls play in the waiting room there?"

"Yeah, I think they would enjoy that, at least for a little while."

"Sounds good to me." I wiped a drop of milk from Darika's chin with the corner of her bib. "How was Angelika this morning?"

"She seems to be doing pretty well. She has quite the grip! When I put my finger in there, she just wrapped her hand around it and wouldn't let go."

The thought of those miniature fingers wrapped around her daddy's large one made me smile. Untying Darika's bib, I said, "Looks like we're ready to go over now."

"All right, Alisha, are you ready to go?" Galen dumped the paper bowls and napkins into the trash and reached to take Darika from me. "Let's go." Alisha took my hand, and we headed for the elevator.

The day passed quickly. Galen spent most of his time keeping Darika entertained, while Alisha played with several other small children in the family waiting room. I enjoyed some quality time with Angelika.

"How's my little girl today?" I asked softly as I cupped my hand over her. We weren't allowed to touch her much yet because she was easily over-stimulated, but we often cradled her with our hands just a little, so that she could feel we were there.

"I think you are growing," I noted happily. It was hard to see progress sometimes, but she looked just a wee bit bigger, somehow. I couldn't wait until I could hold her!

The nurse came over to do the routine assessment she completed every two hours. "Hello, Esther," she greeted me cheerfully. "How are you today?"

"Pretty good."

"Good." I watched as she moved in gently and began talking softly as she worked. "Hello, Angelika. How's my baby girl? Yes, we're just going to do a little check-up again." She slipped her stethoscope into her ears to listen to Angelika's heart and lungs. "We're just going to see what we can hear," she crooned. I could tell by her tender manner that she really cared about Angelika.

When she had finished her head-to-toe check, she looked over at me and smiled. "She's doing pretty well today. We'll just keep taking it a day at a time. Won't we, sweetie?" She stroked Angelika's tiny fingers before removing her hands from the isolette. "You and Galen are awesome parents."

I blushed a little. "We couldn't do any less."

"Well, this baby is being loved into this world, that's for sure." She nodded emphatically. "Keep it up." She turned to go, and I turned my attention back to Angelika.

"Angelika, Mama's here with you. Mama loves you." I reached in and held my finger close to her hand. She grasped it firmly and hung on. Her skinny little legs were crossed. I counted the precious wee toes on the one little foot encased in the bit of bandage that held an I.V.

Her face was almost entirely covered by the taped ventilator tube, and a pink hat band covered the eyes that had never yet opened to the light. Only her miniature nose peeped out. I avoided looking too long at her skinny tummy that seemed to be all ribs.

Her fingers tightened even more on my finger as I moved slightly. It was almost as if she were telling me not to leave her. "It's okay, Angelika. Mama's not going away." The beeps of the ventilator mingled with the many sounds of the NICU.

I glanced at the clock and saw it was 5:00. I had another half hour before I would have to leave.

I looked up at the monitor above her bed. In these first few weeks Galen and I had become nearly addicted to watching the monitors whenever we were with Angelika. They gave us just a little glimpse into how she was doing. I was slowly learning to decipher the basic meanings of the various graphs and numbers. Right now her oxygen saturation was at 92. The ideal setting was 100. But it jumped around so frequently that it could go from 88 to 98 within several seconds' time. The beeping alarm went off only if it went below 85.

As I watched her heart rate, I noticed it jump when someone dropped something in the adjoining pod. I was pleased to see that Angelika was responding to her surroundings. Glancing at the vent monitor, I traced the squiggly green line that represented her breathing. There was a little purple line mingling with the green, and I noted it with pleasure. That purple line represented the breaths she was taking independently of the ventilator. At the moment, the vent was set at twenty-four breaths per minute, and she was breathing twenty-six times per minute.

"Angelika, Mama will come back. I'm not going to leave you for very long. I love you, Angelika." I always hated this part of the visit, when I had to tear myself away from her. Silently I prayed, committing her to the care of our heavenly Father as we did every time we left her. "Mama loves you," I whispered as I turned to go with a lump in my throat.

Galen was just coming back from a walk in the hall with the girls. Always good-natured and calm, he hardly seemed tired by his long afternoon with two active little ones. He smiled at me over Darika's head. "Ready to go for supper?"

Later as I held Darika and sang her to sleep, my weary heart was soothed. My other babies needed me too, and Angelika was in good hands. I would just have to keep reminding myself of this. I didn't know if that realization would make it any easier to leave Angelika each day, especially as she got older and was more aware of our presence or absence. For tonight, though, I was just grateful to have Darika and Alisha with us.

By the end of the week, we had fallen into a sort of routine. Galen spent a lot of time entertaining the girls. With the imminent arrival of spring, he started taking them on walks outdoors. We both tried to spend time daily with Angelika, and it seemed that she was making good progress. It felt as though maybe, finally, we were starting to settle in. This would potentially be home for months to come, and it felt good to be living a bit more normally again after the past three weeks' major upheaval. In time, however, I was to learn that in a situation like ours, a "normal" manner of living did not exist. And in the midst of the uncertainties, I was to learn in a whole new way what it meant to be carried by God's grace, moment by moment.

10 Precious Firsts

—*Esther*

I glanced around at the familiar faces of our home congregation as I made my way to one of the back benches. Alisha climbed up beside me and I settled Darika on my lap just as the first song number was given. This was our first Sunday back at Summersville since Angelika's arrival, and it felt so right to be with our church family again.

Smiling, the lady sitting beside me slid closer to share her hymn book with me. "It's good to have you back!" she whispered.

We began to sing, and the music swelled and rang out exultantly. "There is, beyond the azure blue, a God concealed from human sight . . . There is a God; He is alive! In Him we live, and we survive . . ."

I was glad we hadn't let the eight inches of late snow or Darika's slight fever keep us from coming today. I felt my spirits lifting as we sang. I knew Galen needed the encouragement too. He had been asked to lead the devotional meditation that morning, and he focused on recounting God's faithfulness.

"It's so good to be back with home folks again," he began. "Thank you to each one who has been a support to us in the last few weeks. We've been much in need of your prayers, and we have certainly felt them carrying us.

"Since Angelika's birth almost a month ago, much has happened. Through it all, God has been unceasingly faithful. Let's turn to Lamentations 3:22-25."

Pages rustled softly throughout the room as people found the reference. I opened a small container of Cheerios for Darika and gave Alisha a notepad and pen to keep her occupied before turning my attention back to Galen.

> It is of the LORD's mercies that we are not consumed, because his compassions fail not. They are new every morning: great is thy faithfulness. The LORD is my portion, saith my soul; therefore will I hope in him. The LORD is good unto them that wait for him, to the soul that seeketh him.

"We have certainly discovered the truth of this passage in a deeper way in the last weeks. God's grace is there on a daily basis. We have often sensed His leading and His presence in the midst of difficult circumstances. His mercy and faithfulness leave me feeling small but amazingly loved. I feel so unworthy but privileged to be shown His care in such a powerful way on a personal level.

"The words, 'The LORD is my portion, saith my soul' were a comforting thought to me last week. We again faced the possibility of losing Angelika and the potential of long-term damage if the swelling didn't go down. Somehow, in the midst of all that, just knowing that God was in control brought such peace. No matter what happens, God is there for us."

As we drove back toward the city that snowy afternoon, Galen and I discussed the morning service. "I think they appreciated hearing a bit of an update and a testimony from us in person," Galen noted. "As we were leaving, one of the men thanked me for sharing. He said that it somehow made the whole situation seem more real to hear it directly from us. It also does me good to get out and focus on other people. We're not the only ones facing difficult circumstances, and we might be able to bring encouragement to others. I think our testimony can bring God glory if we let it."

I nodded thoughtfully as I gazed at the swirling whiteness outside the window. "Galen, sometimes I feel like asking why all this is happening. But when you put it like that, it makes more sense. Still, when I see all the pain our baby has to go through, I can't see the positive side of it all very well."

"It's not easy," he agreed softly. "But we have to keep looking to God and trusting that He does have a purpose, whether we can see it or not."

I turned in my seat to wipe Darika's nose. Her forehead felt hot against my palm. "Are we taking the girls up to Lon's place tonight? She still has a fever."

"I guess we'll have to leave them there for a day or two." Galen glanced in his rearview mirror at the two little girls sitting restlessly in their car seats. "We can't keep them at the Ronald McDonald House when they're sick."

"I wonder if it's not just that she's teething. I'm pretty sure that's what is causing her symptoms." But I knew we couldn't take the chance, even if I hated to part with them again so soon. Sick children were not allowed at the Ronald McDonald House for good reasons, and we wanted to respect that.

Alisha squirmed in her seat. "I'm hungry, Mama!" she complained. As I reached for a pretzel stick to give her, Darika started to fuss.

"Should I put some music on?" Galen asked.

"Yeah, let's try it. Hopefully they'll fall asleep soon." I reached back and stroked Darika's hand.

The girls soon calmed and listened contentedly to the soft, harmonizing voices that filled the air. The words of a hymn caught my attention. "What a fellowship, what a joy divine, leaning on the everlasting arms . . . safe and secure from all alarms." Mentally I pictured the card friends had given us after one of our miscarriages several years ago. On the front was the painting of a lighthouse, half hidden by lashing waves and surrounded by a raging storm, yet bravely sending out a feeble glow of light. Above it, the skies were black. Lightning split the clouds. Out of this stormy turmoil, God's strong hands reached out to shelter the lonely lighthouse. Below the painting were the words from Deuteronomy 33:27: "And underneath are the everlasting arms."

The next verse was playing. "What have I to dread, what have I to fear, leaning on the everlasting arms?" I knew God was speaking to my heart. Though we had faced many fearful storms in the past few weeks and would probably face many more, He would be there in the midst of them as He had so faithfully proven in the past. He seemed to whisper, "Lean on me. You have nothing to fear. I am here and I will carry you."

The NICU was quieter than usual that evening as I watched Angelika. Her feet were crossed, and she looked at rest. I enjoyed these moments when she seemed entirely peaceful. I noticed that she had crossed her hands over her chest too. She had been opening her eyes more and more of late. She opened them now and peered blearily up at her plastic world. They soon closed again and she seemed to resume her nap.

Icy was on duty that night. She came over and asked softly, "How is Angelika tonight?"

"She's relaxed right now." I smiled at Icy appreciatively. We had learned that she always prayed for the babies in her care. Watching her gentle manner as she cared for Angelika gave us total confidence that her heart was as genuine as her radiant smile conveyed.

"Would you like to kangaroo tonight?" she questioned as she slipped her stethoscope into her ears.

"Yes, I would," I replied, my heart quickening at the prospect of holding our little girl for the first time. She was now almost one month old.

Kangarooing, or skin-to-skin contact, was proven to be good for preemie babies in most situations. The thought of actually being able to do something for our baby made my heart swell with hope. They had told us a week and a half before that we might be able to hold her soon, but it hadn't been mentioned again until this evening.

I held my breath as I watched Icy lift the tiny form from the incubator. Angelika's arms and legs flailed as Icy cradled her in her hands. Gently, Icy placed her on my chest, and I reached out to cradle her with one hand.

Feeling the small form against my heart nearly took my breath away. Her slight form rose and fell with my breathing as I relaxed. I marveled as I felt the tiny hands against my chest. Looking down at her masked face and feeling her legs pull up against me, I felt overwhelmed. It was so wonderful to actually be holding her!

As I sat and held her, my heart was stirred with a deep longing to protect this helpless life from all the pain and trauma that she was facing. Softly I crooned her name. "Mama loves you, precious baby. God has special plans for you, and He loves you very much." I wondered what kind of a future she would have.

For forty-five minutes, I savored this precious bonding time. Then Angelika got restless, and Icy decided it was time to put her back. "It's her way of saying, 'This has been good, but I'm ready to go back to bed now,' " she explained. "You did so well and she seemed to like it. We'll have to do it again soon."

I agreed. It was a wonderful milestone, and I would never forget the feeling of that feather-light form nestled close to my heart.

11 Reaching Out

—Galen

"So how's it going for you folks?" I asked as I took a seat across from Ben in the Ronald McDonald living room. We had quickly become friends with Ben and Liz in those first few weeks at the hospital, and we often stopped to talk to each other when our paths crossed.

"Oh, it's going okay," Ben sighed. "It was one of those days when you wish you could get out for a walk in the woods and regain some sanity, but I really can't complain." He shifted in his seat and straightened his camouflage cap.

"I know what you mean. There's always someone who has it worse than we do," I agreed.

"That's for sure. How is Angelika?"

"She was up and down today, but she's doing all right. We're really thankful she's doing as well as she is. All the uncertainty really gets to you after a while."

Ben nodded. "Just when you think you're making

progress, you lose ground. Sometimes I wonder why bad things happen to good people. Liz and I haven't really lived what one could call a religious life, but we're basically good people. I just don't quite understand why God puts good people through things like this. It seems unfair."

I listened thoughtfully. "That's a good question, Ben. I think a lot of people ask that sort of thing when they face difficult circumstances. Your view of God will shape what conclusions you come to."

"You think so? How do you view God?" Ben looked interested.

"Well, I think in a situation like ours, it's especially important to realize that God is a God of love. He's sovereign and in control of everything, but He's not out to hurt people. His desire is to have a personal relationship with every individual, and He cares what happens in each of our lives."

"If He cares so much, why does He allow bad things to happen?"

"Often He has purposes that we can't see. Sometimes He's trying to get our attention so that we'll respond to His call on our lives. Ben, there are a lot of things in life I don't understand either, and I don't want to pretend that I do understand them. But there is one thing I'm convinced of. When we become His children through a personal relationship with Jesus Christ, He works all things together for our good no matter what happens.

"When you know God, it somehow changes everything. Then your purpose and end isn't really found here on this earth anyway, and your goal becomes knowing and serving Him. And with the promise of eternity in heaven, this earthly life doesn't seem nearly as important. In the end, where we'll spend eternity is really all that matters."

"I see your point. But as I said, I'm not really big into that religious stuff. I know God exists and I could probably be a better person than I am, but I can't see giving my whole life to it like you're talking about."

"How do you view God, Ben?"

He grinned good-naturedly. "Awww, I don't know. I know He exists. I've always been interested in the Native American's religious views. You know how they call Him the Great Spirit."

"Do you really think the Great Spirit is God?" I asked.

"Why not?" He shrugged. "Aren't they all the same? I've always thought that all the religions probably shared the same God. It doesn't really matter what you call Him."

"I think that depends on what you base truth on. What defines truth?"

"I guess I'm really not sure I ever thought of that before." Ben's eyes were thoughtful.

"Do you think the Bible is a solid basis for truth?"

"Perhaps. I don't know. We're getting pretty deep here." Ben chuckled. Despite the serious nature of our conversation, I found myself grinning with him.

"Through all the ages, the Bible has remained unchanged, and it is applicable to everyone from every walk of life, no matter what their race or station might be. It was inspired by God's Spirit, and it's God's own message to us."

Ben shrugged. "I don't know. I guess it's all in what a person chooses to believe. I respect people like you, but that's more religion than I care for. I do think I might try to find a church to go to when this whole thing is over, though."

The conversation moved on to other things, and we soon decided it was time to turn in for the night. But Ben's questions went with me. I really cared about and respected the Turners, and I felt burdened for them. As I fell asleep, I prayed that God would give Ben the answers he was seeking and that he and Liz would find Him.

One day we met a middle-aged couple named Abe and Lori. We discovered they were both paramedics, and Abe had just returned from serving in Afghanistan. They were helping care for their unmarried daughter's child, who was born with severe heart complications. We enjoyed getting to know them, and Lori took a special interest in our girls.

"Look, Daddy." Alisha held up the picture of a kitten she was coloring.

"Very pretty, Alisha. Did you say 'thank you' to Lori?" I smiled at the motherly woman sitting beside her. "They really enjoy the coloring books you bring for them. It sure helps pass the time."

"They're such good children," she replied softly. "I'm sure the hours get very long for them sometimes."

"Yes, any diversion that keeps them occupied is good." I turned to Abe. "How are things going with the baby?"

"Oh, she's doing as well as can be expected, I think," Abe replied. He ran his hand over his hair. "As you like to say, we take it a day at a time and trust that things will work out one way or another in the end."

I nodded. "I certainly know what you mean there,

Abe. It takes a lot of faith to get through these sorts of circumstances."

"Yeah, it does take believing in something outside of yourself. That became especially real to me when I was overseas. Some of the things I saw left me thinking about life and death and what happens after."

"And none of us is guaranteed another day. That's why it's so important to know where you are going."

Abe looked at me thoughtfully. "Do you feel like you know where you're going?" he asked curiously.

"Yes, I do. But there isn't anything I can do to earn my salvation. I could never be good enough."

Abe grinned slightly. "You seem pretty good to me."

I shook my head. "No one is ever good enough to approach God on the grounds of his own goodness. We all sin, and it separates us from God. Only through the death of Christ was this barrier removed. That's why believing in Christ's sacrifice is so important. It's the only way to truly know God. Even though I was raised in a Christian home, it wasn't until I turned from my sin to follow Christ that I had peace with God and knew that I was forgiven and headed for heaven."

Abe's eyes had a faraway look as I finished. After a moment of silence, he looked up. "I think I know what you mean, Galen. In my field I've seen many men die, and there's a strong difference between those who die knowing God and those who don't."

On numerous occasions we discussed our beliefs and what it meant to truly know God. These discussions nurtured a friendship that lasted even after we both left the hospital.

During those first weeks of our hospital stay, we often glimpsed a young Amish couple who also had a preemie baby there. Though we did not connect much in those first days due to their quiet personalities, I felt a growing burden for their souls. I sensed they had religion but lacked the freedom and joy of a personal relationship with Christ.

Late one night, after most everyone else had gone to bed, I happened to meet Joel in the hall as he returned from going out to smoke. Feeling that perhaps this was the opportunity I had been waiting for, I struck up a conversation with him.

"So how is your baby?" I asked.

"Good," he replied. "Growing like a little weed. And you have a baby here too?"

I nodded. "Yes, our Angelika is over a month old now, and she's doing well."

The conversation drifted to what we did for a living. He worked in a cabinet shop and farmed on the side. I told him I farmed poultry for a living. As we discussed farming, the talk turned to our roots. I began to ask him about how their group did things and what they believed.

Though friendly, he was guarded and seemed to avoid going too deep.

"Do you think that salvation has to do with our works?" I asked.

He shrugged. "One can't be sure."

"How do you know?" I asked. "Doesn't the Bible say that the only way to God is through Jesus Christ?"

He shrugged again and shifted uncomfortably on the sofa. "We believe that worldliness separates us from God," he replied pointedly. "I've noticed that you drive a car. How do you justify that?"

"I do agree that worldliness is something that separates us from God. I respect those who choose the simple lifestyle, but I feel that worldliness is more a heart condition than anything else. I don't think driving a car necessarily makes you worldly. It's where your heart lies—becoming proud or trusting in your possessions is what makes a person worldly, as I understand it.

"But the Bible clearly tells us that religion, good works, or a strict lifestyle can't save us. These things are good and even right. But it's only through the forgiveness of Christ in our lives and a personal relationship with Him that we can truly have salvation."

Joel cocked his head slightly. "We just have to do our best to keep the rules and live right, and then we can hope to get into heaven."

"In Acts, when the Philippian jailor asked Paul, 'What must I do to be saved?' they told him, 'Believe on the Lord Jesus Christ, and thou shalt be saved.' From that I see that we can have assurance of salvation. God doesn't want us to live in doubt and fear all our lives. He sent Christ to sacrifice His life so that we could have life more abundantly. He came to set us free from the law of sin and death. He replaced this with a personal relationship of obedience to Christ and His Holy Spirit in our lives."

Joel shrugged and changed the subject. Though we parted on friendly terms, he showed little interest in what I had shared with him. Still, the seed was planted. Perhaps he would think about it later. I knew only God could open Joel's eyes to his need for Him.

There were times when we felt too caught up in our own pain to reach out, and many times we felt that we received more than we gave. One night a couple who had a small child with a disfigured face came over to talk to us. As we shared stories, we discovered that they were believers as well. When they found out why we were there, they asked if they could pray with us. Their compassion stemmed from their own journey through hospital stays, bills, and all the uncertainty that goes with a situation like that. Our hearts were blessed by their sweet, caring attitude.

We felt we had been called to a mission field during the months we spent in the hospital. Truly, the opportunities to reach out were innumerable. We saw so many who didn't have the love of Christ in their lives, and our hearts ached for them. How could people face difficult circumstances without the security of His love and the confidence of His care? Through it all, our desire was to be used of God in whatever way He saw fit to reach out to burdened souls in this place of tears and pain.

12 No Matter What, God Loves Me!

—Esther

My pen scrawled across the lined page as I sat beside Angelika's incubator, recording another day's events in our little black journal. We wanted to document everything significant that happened during Angelika's journey at the hospital. It was March 25, and Dr. Foley had just talked with us about performing an ileostomy on Angelika.

Dr. Foley had installed Angelika's Penrose drain, and we had grown to trust him. He had explained to us that the ileostomy would allow them to start gavage, or tube feeding. Angelika seemed to have a blockage somewhere, and they needed to do something to help her absorb nutrients.

Angelika's ileostomy surgery was scheduled for two days from now. She was stable this afternoon, resting on her tummy comfortably. She now weighed in at 1 pound 10 ounces.

Closing the journal, I laid my pen aside and wiped a bit of

ink from my fingers. Leaning forward, I watched my baby thoughtfully as she stirred in her sleep. Her face screwed up into a silent cry, and I reached in to comfort her. "Angelika, Mama's here." She seemed to calm at the sound of my voice and opened her eyes, blinking sleepily.

As I anticipated the surgery, my heart felt heavy. Must she go through more? It was so hard to watch the pain and discomfort our baby already had to face on a daily basis. I hated to watch when they suctioned her mouth and throat due to the mucous buildup from the ventilator. She always cried and gagged when they did it. Worse, though, was the torn skin on her face where they had to constantly retape her ventilator tube. Tears pricked my eyes as I thought of the added pain that surgery would cause.

Lord, why does she have to hurt so much? my heart asked silently. One of the Bible verses Galen had taped up on the side of Angelika's isolette caught my eye.

"We are troubled on every side, yet not distressed; we are perplexed, but not in despair; persecuted, but not forsaken; cast down, but not destroyed" (2 Corinthians 4:8-9).

Above that, in bold black lettering, were the words taped up for us by one of the nurses: "No matter what, GOD LOVES ME!"

I was grateful for the reminder that God did love Angelika. He loved her even more than we did. No matter how much pain she faced or how much distress and trouble we faced, He was with us in the midst of it and would not forsake us. Sighing, I cuddled her gently with my hands and prayed for grace to trust Him even when I didn't understand what was going on or why.

The next day Galen's parents came down and picked

up the girls for us. They took them to Lon's house, since Angelika's surgery was scheduled for the next morning and we both wanted to be at the hospital.

Late that night after trying all day to get a chance to hold Angelika, they let me kangaroo her. As I cuddled her fragile form against me, I had to blink back tears. She was so precious. I longed just to hold her close and protect her forever.

And then we had to leave. But first, Galen and I placed our hands over the little form inside her isolette as Galen prayed softly. He prayed for peace and for God's hands to guide the surgeon as he performed the surgery the next morning. "You have good plans for us, Lord. Thank you that Angelika is safe in your care." I knew we could trust God implicitly, but it was still hard to leave Angelika alone, knowing what the following day would hold.

Our room back at the Ronald McDonald House seemed quiet without Alisha and Darika. I sat down wearily on the bed and pulled off my socks. "Why is it always so hard to go to bed without the girls?" I wondered aloud.

"I suppose they give us a sense of normality," Galen said. "It's never the same without their happy chatter and cuddling before sleep time."

"Oh, by the way, I want to put addresses on the birth announcements while we sit in the waiting room tomorrow. Don't let me forget to take them," I said.

"I'll put them by the door."

"Okay, thank you." I stifled a splitting yawn with the back of my hand and flipped back the covers. "When should we get up tomorrow?"

"Well, probably by 8:00 or so. Surgery is scheduled for

11:30. I'll set the alarm on my phone."

The next morning we ate a hurried breakfast and walked to the hospital through the chilly air. Heading directly up to the NICU, we scrubbed and went back to see Angelika.

We stood for some time, simply watching her as she lay sleeping in her isolette. One hand was thrown out beside her, palm upward in a relaxed gesture, and the other fist curled under her chin. Her legs and feet were partially hidden by a soft white blanket tucked around her. Rising and falling in quick, short breaths, her chest kept time to the beeping of the ventilator.

As I thought back over the journey of the past weeks, I wondered how many more such weeks lay ahead of us. I tried to imagine the day when we could take our baby girl home with us for good. I still wondered if that day would really ever come. With effort, I reminded myself that it was important to simply live each day with God's grace surrounding me.

The time for surgery came and went. The surgery team was running late and wouldn't be available until later in the afternoon. This gave Galen and me more time with Angelika. We spent some time praying together before they were ready to take her. As we watched her go, I felt a tightness in my chest. *God, please watch over my baby,* my heart pleaded.

Surgery finally started at 2:30. They had told us they expected it to take a little over an hour, and we settled ourselves in the waiting room.

Dr. Foley had explained to us that they would bring a loop of the small intestine through the skin on the right-hand side of the abdomen, bringing the bowel to the outside temporarily. This was what they called the ileostomy. Waste would be collected in an external pouching system stuck to the skin. This would enable them to begin tube feedings within a week or two. When she was older, they would surgically reverse the temporary ileostomy, repairing the loop of intestine that formed the temporary opening in the skin. The goal was that the intestines would then perform normally inside her body.

Time moved slowly. I glanced out the window at the busy street below and then around the waiting room at our neighbors. To our left, a middle-aged man sat idly flipping through a magazine. He glanced at his watch from time to time. Next to him, a mother tried to keep her active toddler quiet, and I wondered how Alisha and Darika were doing. Across the room from us, a young woman sat with her head in her hands. She seemed to have no companions in the vicinity, and I wondered what sorrow weighed her down. Quietly I prayed that God would reach out and touch her in the midst of her need. Glancing at the clock again, I noted that it would still be at least twenty minutes before Angelika came out of surgery.

I finished addressing all of the birth announcements. As I put them back into my bag, I noticed an envelope I hadn't opened yet from yesterday's mail.

Flipping the card open, I read, "May you feel the unfailing strength of the Lord during this time of difficulty and trial. He wants to 'bear you on eagles' wings' (Exodus 19:4)."

"Galen, do you want to read this?" I handed it to him and watched his face as he read.

He looked up. "God always brings just what we need when we need it, doesn't He?"

"He does, and we have so much to be thankful for. Even

in the lowest, hardest times, His grace has been there to carry us through another day."

"And His people have certainly been a great means of encouragement too."

Finally Dr. Foley came out to talk to us. His eyes were smiling under the green surgeon's cap pulled low on his forehead. "Well, we have good news. The surgery was uneventful and things look good. It took us longer than I had predicted because there was more scar tissue than I was anticipating. We were able to leave 60 centimeters of bowel inside, which is plenty for digestive purposes. We did give a transfusion, but that's quite normal too."

Galen had been able to donate blood for Angelika before the surgery, for which I was grateful. It felt much safer for her to receive his blood instead of a stranger's. He had told me that it felt special to be able to do this for his baby, helping her in a tangible way. I could identify, having had the opportunity to kangaroo her. So often we simply felt helpless.

A little while later, we went in to see Angelika. Her color was good and she was resting quietly. As I watched her, a great sense of relief washed over me. One more hurdle had been conquered, and she had come through well. I reached in to stroke her fingers and blinked back tears of relief. *Thank you, God,* my heart whispered.

At 4:00 a.m. the nurse on duty noted that Angelika's blood pressure was alarmingly low. She realized that the situation was serious and called for a nurse practitioner. She well knew that when the flow of blood was too low to

deliver enough oxygen and nutrients to the vital organs, those organs could not function normally and were at risk of both temporary and permanent damage.

"She's dehydrating. That's what is causing her blood pressure to drop so drastically," the nurse practitioner diagnosed.

At 8:00 the ringing of Galen's cell phone woke us. I listened as Galen answered. "She is? Oh, no! Okay, we'll be over soon."

Suddenly wide awake, I asked Galen, "What's wrong?"

"It was one of the nurse practitioners. She said Angelika took a turn for the worse early this morning. Her blood pressure has dropped alarmingly, and they are having difficulty getting it back up."

"Let's go." I felt an urgent desire to be with my baby.

"We'll go over as soon as we can get ready, but let's pray first. And then I'm going to call the prayer chains and let them know what's going on," Galen decided.

Despite the desperate feeling of urgency, I knew there was nothing better we could do at the moment than stop and take our need to God. As we prayed, the tension inside softened just a bit.

By the time Galen made the prayer chain phone calls and we had prepared for the day, it was nearly 9:00. When we reached the NICU, we scrubbed quickly and wended our way back to Angelika's isolette. Her nurse looked up as we approached and smiled. "It looks like we have good news for you. She stabilized about twenty minutes ago." I heaved a big sigh of relief.

As Galen and I exchanged a relieved smile, it suddenly hit us. Angelika had stabilized around the same time as the prayer chains finished going around. God had answered the prayers of His people almost instantly! We were humbled and awed by His amazing goodness to us yet again.

13 *Emergency Surgery*

—Galen

I awoke Tuesday morning just as the pale light of a gray dawn crept through the cracks in the window shade. The heavy rumble of a passing truck and the sharp blare of a car horn reminded me that the city had never gone to sleep, but with daylight the noise volume always increased considerably. Sleepily I wondered what day it was and remembered Esther commenting the night before that it was the last day in March. Was it really April already? So much had happened in the last six weeks. It felt like a long time since life had been normal.

I lay still for some time, thinking about the past week. After her crisis, Angelika seemed to be doing a bit better. For that we felt grateful. I let my mind wander to the duties at home. The chores had gone well since we had left, due to the capable help of my nephews. With April upon us, I needed to do my taxes in the next few days, maybe even tomorrow. If I went to the hospital now, I'd have time to spend an hour or so with Angelika yet before breakfast. Yawning, I pushed back the covers and slipped out of bed.

When I reached Angelika, she was restless. "Angelika, Daddy loves you. How is my girl today? You're getting bigger!" I stood talking to her and held her tiny hand in mine. The night nurse was just getting ready to leave. I asked her how Angelika had been through the night.

"Oh, she did okay. She's still trying to get on top after that surgery, of course, but she's hanging in there. She's a tough little girl, that's for sure." She nodded for emphasis.

As the nurse turned to leave, I reached back into the isolette and stroked Angelika's head with my fingertips. "How are you feeling, sweetheart? You're a little fighter! Grow big and strong so we can take you home soon." The words sounded a little silly, since I knew we still had a long road ahead of us before we'd be able to take her home. But I said the words to foster hope in my own heart. She'd been through a lot of low moments in the last few weeks, and sometimes it was easy to feel discouraged. Our goal looked so far away. We hoped that maybe by the time her due date arrived in mid-June, we could take her home. But that was still several months away, and there was no guarantee that she'd be ready even then.

"I guess we just need to have patience each day," I reminded myself aloud. "God's grace is here for today. And He is watching over you, little one. You just rest and get well, okay? You're in good hands. We'll keep trusting that God knows what's best for you." She was resting a bit easier now, but she still seemed uncomfortable. I continued to talk to her softly with her hand in mine until she fell asleep.

When I got back to our room, Esther was up and getting the girls ready for the day. Darika was lying on the bed on her tummy. When she saw me, she started scooting herself toward the edge of the bed. "Where are you going?" I chuckled as I scooped her up. "You're just getting all over the place, aren't you? Pretty soon you'll be running around with Alisha." I kissed her fuzzy head and smiled down at Alisha, who was impatiently shifting from one foot to the other while Esther finished combing her hair.

"She really is getting around now," Esther agreed. "Sometimes I just cringe at how dirty she gets, though, crawling through the halls. Her knees are black by the end of the day." She shook her head disconcertedly. "Sometimes I feel like such a bad mother. How does she ever come up with all that dirt?"

"It'll be okay, Esther. You're doing the best you can, and that's all you can do. A little bit of dirt probably won't hurt her," I comforted.

Turning toward Alisha, I tugged her pigtail playfully. "Are you ready for some breakfast?" I asked.

"Yes!" She giggled.

Esther reached for Darika. "I just need to change my squirming bundle of energy yet, and then we can go."

The day passed uneventfully until around 6:00 that evening when I went to see Angelika again. Her tummy looked swollen. The nurse told me Angelika's day had been rather rough. "Her white blood cell count has been trending up all day, which is a marker of infection. We've called Dr. Fallat to come up and check on her." I could tell she was worried.

Dr. Fallat arrived shortly. As chief of pediatric surgery,

she had a capable air. Quickly she assessed the situation and ordered a CT scan of the swollen abdomen.

At this point, things began to escalate. Angelika was running a fever and her stomach bloated even more. I waited anxiously for word on the diagnosis. Around 9:00, a resident doctor came over to talk to me. "We are looking at a case of intestinal ischemia and infarction," he announced. Seeing my blank face, he hastened to explain that part of Angelika's intestine had died due to a decrease in its blood supply.

"Intestinal ischemia is a serious condition that must be treated promptly or it can result in death. Although the outlook depends on what caused the condition, prompt treatment is the only means of achieving a good outcome."

"What type of treatment are they proposing?" I asked, trying to wrap my mind around the information I had just received.

"Under the present circumstances, emergency surgery is your only option," he told me decidedly. "They'll remove the section of intestine that died and reconnect the healthy, remaining ends of bowel. They will also attempt to correct the blockage of arteries supplying the intestine, if at all possible."

I did not hesitate. It seemed our only avenue, and I felt at peace with doing whatever could be done. "We'll go ahead with the surgery then," I agreed.

"Good. We'll get things under way as soon as possible." With a quick nod, he strode away. I went to call Esther.

My fingers shook a little as I dialed the number. Esther answered on the first ring.

"Honey, this is Galen." I had notified her earlier that

Angelika wasn't doing very well and that I didn't know what we could expect as the evening wore on, so she was waiting for my call. Still, neither of us was prepared for what was happening now.

"Is everything all right?"

"No. They've decided Angelika needs emergency surgery yet tonight. Please call someone to come stay with the girls right away so you can meet me here as soon as you can."

Esther didn't stop to ask questions. "Okay, I'll call Lon's right now." I hung up the phone and prayed.

By 11:00 p.m. the surgical team was ready to start. My mom had come down with Lon and Leona to be with us during the surgery. We watched outside the glass windows of the small room where they were prepping Angelika. I slipped my arm around Esther. Her eyes were shiny with unshed tears, and I knew she was struggling with the suddenness of it all.

We watched the masked doctors hovering over Angelika's tiny, bloated form. The harshness of the lights made the room look cold and stark, and she looked so utterly helpless.

"She looks so cold," Esther whispered. I heard the catch in her voice and took her hand.

"We need to remember that she's still in God's care. She's safe there." But it didn't feel that way. When they were ready to begin the surgery, we settled in the family waiting room.

"So what happened?" my mom questioned. She had not yet been informed of what was really going on.

We explained what intestinal ischemia and infarction meant. "They said there are several things that could have contributed to it, including her bout with low blood pressure the day after surgery. It's a pretty serious condition, but they hope for a good outcome since they got onto it right away."

"Did you call the prayer chains?" Esther asked.

"Yes, I did. It seems we've been calling them a lot in the last few weeks, doesn't it?"

"It does feel as though there have been more crisis moments the last while," Esther agreed, sighing. "I don't know if we'd make it without all their prayers."

"Could we pray together right now?" my mom requested.

"Sure, let's do that," I agreed. We quietly bowed our heads and prayed as the clock ticked on toward midnight.

The hands on the clock seemed to fall asleep as time dragged on. My eyelids felt heavy and I fought to stay awake. At last I dozed lightly.

When Dr. Fallat came in to talk to us, I glanced blearily at the clock and saw that it was 1:45 in the morning. Blinking the sleep from my eyes, I noted that the surgeon looked weary but relieved. She said that the surgery had gone as well as could be expected, but only time would tell whether the outcome would be successful. At least for now our baby was out of danger.

"You are welcome to go see her yet tonight if you like," the surgeon added before leaving.

We walked mechanically into the hall, dizzy with sleep. Slowly my mind cleared, and I felt a bit more alert by the time we arrived at the door to the room where Angelika was in recovery.

She was still sedated but looked peaceful. We decided to wait just a bit longer until she was more alert before going back to the Ronald McDonald House for the night.

"You two look totally beat," my mom commented sympathetically.

"Well, I do feel a little as though someone's been beating up on me." I cracked a grin and Mom laughed softly. It felt good to break the tension after all we had faced that evening. And it was such a relief to know that Angelika had pulled through yet another surgery.

By the time Angelika came around, it was nearly 3:00. When we were certain she was all right, we left and wearily made our way to our room. After a grateful good night to the rather sleepy but gracious Lon and Leona, who had been staying with the girls, they and Mom left for home. Esther and I crept under the covers and fell into a deep sleep.

14 Dolphins and Family Prayers

—Galen

We entered the dim interior of the small room. Alisha grabbed my hand tightly and whispered, "Where are the dolphins, Daddy?" I glanced around at the few people already seated toward the front of the room. The enormous IMAX screen, aglow with a pale light, was blank.

"They'll be up there in just a little while," I told her, pointing to the screen. "Let's find a seat." I led her into the very back row of seats and helped her into one. Sitting down next to her, I settled Darika on my lap and scanned the back of a brochure I had picked up on our way in.

> It's rare to watch an IMAX film at the Louisville Science Center without grabbing your armrests at least once because the motion on the screen creates the sensation of moving in your seat. The sheer size of the screen provides incredible visuals and,

along with the enhanced sound, makes it nearly impossible for little ones to lose interest for too long during the show.

I certainly hope they're right, I thought wryly. Darika had taken off with her crawling and loved to be on the move constantly. Earlier in the week when the girls were feeling especially restless with being cooped up, I'd decided on a trip to the science center. I knew Alisha would love the science film about dolphins, but I still didn't feel entirely certain just how well Darika would sit for it.

The lights dimmed even more. The sound of crashing surf filled the room, and I sensed Alisha's excitement mounting. Then suddenly the screen came alive with sporting dolphins and ocean spray. I looked down at her and smiled as I watched her eyes follow their every movement, a look of wonder growing on her upturned face. Darika also seemed mesmerized by all the movement and noise. I relaxed in my seat, ready to take in the interesting presentation on these intriguing creatures.

My relief was short-lived, however. Before many moments had passed, Darika grew restless and began to fuss. At first I tried to distract her with her bottle, but she didn't want that. She wanted to move! I gave in. Taking her behind the seats, I lowered her to the floor. She looked up at me with a lopsided grin of triumph. Daddy had finally understood what she really wanted! Quickly dropping to her hands and knees, she disappeared under the nearest seat to explore. As I watched her drop to her belly to creep underneath, I couldn't help chuckling to myself. I was glad there weren't many people here today. Had it been full, Darika's antics would have proved an undesirable distraction.

Pushing herself backward, Darika reappeared and took off crawling toward the other end of the room. I followed, keeping one eye on Alisha, who still sat entranced, taking everything in. As I chased Darika around for the remainder of the hour, I thought about how life had changed for our family since Angelika's arrival.

Esther and I hadn't talked much about it, but I knew that our experiences of the past months had changed both of us. It had given us both a less temporal perspective. Esther admitted that when others talked about their businesses and hobbies, sometimes it was hard to enter their world anymore. Momentary gain, jobs, and possessions had all lost their value in the light of a precious life on the line.

I felt that we were learning to be less busy and take more time with our children. In a fresh way, this experience had driven home the truth that you can't take anything of earthly value with you in the end, anyway. The only things of eternal value are the souls of those around us. What we invested in our children and the lives of others now was what would truly prove important in light of eternity.

It wasn't that we hadn't cherished our children before this. It was simply that, in our fast-paced culture, it was so easy to become too busy to really take time for the important things. Our sense of what was truly important had grown to new depths, and I prayed that these changes would carry on in our lives even after this crisis was over.

As we left the science museum, Alisha looked up at me with the wonder still lingering in her eyes. "Dolphins are fun. Can we come see them again sometime, Daddy?"

"Maybe." I shifted Darika to my other hip and took

Alisha's hand. "What did you learn today about dolphins?"

"They swim and they squeak," she responded enthusiastically.

"God has created some amazing creatures, hasn't He?"

She nodded. "Did God make the dolphins too?"

"He certainly did. He made all the animals. Remember the story in Genesis about how He created the world?"

"Oh, yes, and Adam too."

We had reached the car now. I smiled down at her as I buckled her into her seat. "That's right, and He made you too."

"And you and Mommy and Darika?"

"Yes, Alisha. And baby Angelika too. God made everybody in the whole world."

"Shall we go to the park tonight?" I asked after supper one evening.

"Yes! Let's go!" Alisha bounced on her chair excitedly.

"That sounds fun." Esther looked up from where she was washing the pizza sauce off Darika's chubby face. "I've been feeling a little restless all afternoon, and I think getting out would help a lot."

Putting the girls into their car seats, we drove down through the city to one of our favorite parks right along the Ohio River. As we left the asphalt and noise behind and entered the quiet paths and spreading shade trees, Esther breathed a deep sigh of relief. I felt my own shoulders relax as well.

We strolled along beside the sloping banks of the river

in the dusky light of the April evening and reveled in the relative quiet. Alisha ran delightedly around us, stopping every now and then to pluck one of the many dandelions that nestled in the lush green grass beside the walk. When we reached a wayside bench, we sat down and watched the river roll away below us.

"It feels so good to get away from the hospital for a little while," Esther said. "It just seems to give me the boost I need to go back and make it through another day. The hospital is a place of sorrow and tears. Sometimes I just ache with all the pain around us. Then sometimes I'm so wrapped up in our own pain that I don't even see anybody else's."

"I know what you mean," I said softly. "The last few months have not been easy ones. But God has been so good to us, and we have so much to be thankful for."

"He really has been. And people have been good to us too. I'm sure we could never repay them all." From somewhere nearby, a bird began twittering its evening song.

"No, we won't ever be able to repay them," I agreed. "But hard experiences have a way of giving you a new level of compassion, and being in a place of need brings a whole new level of appreciation for the love of God's people. That in turn gives you a desire to reach out to others more. I think the time will come when we will have more to give because we've walked through this. I know He's already doing good things in my heart because of it.

"And you know, Esther, I was just thinking earlier this week about how much this whole situation has already changed our perspective and our values. We probably wouldn't be spending nearly so much time with the girls and making memories like this if we weren't stuck here in

Louisville."

"I know, I've been thinking that too. I'm really grateful for the good times we can have."

"It does make discipline a bit more complex, but the girls seem to be doing really well despite everything. They'll probably be more balanced and adjusted to life in the end than they would have been otherwise. They'll be more flexible, anyway."

"Or at least we'll be," Esther laughed.

Alisha came skipping up with her hands full of dandelions. "Here, Mama." She thrust the drooping bouquet into Esther's hand. We both smiled down at her. "Thank you, Alisha. These are very pretty. You know how much Mama likes flowers, don't you?"

She nodded, climbing up between us and nestling close to Esther. "Can we get ice cream?"

We exchanged glances, and I looked at my watch. "If we go now, I think we'll have time yet before we have to take them home to bed," I decided. We had gone to the park the week before and stopped for ice cream on the way home, and Alisha obviously hadn't forgotten it.

"Life is too short not to stop for ice cream," Esther said. We grinned at each other.

Darika was stirring in her stroller and blinked up at me sleepily as she awoke. "I bet Darika wants ice cream too, don't you?" I patted her head. "Okay, let's go." Getting to our feet, we strolled back toward the car in the gathering dusk.

After the girls had both been washed up from their sticky treat and were in their pajamas for the night, we gathered for family prayers. We knelt in a circle. Alisha bowed her head and closed her eyes tight while Darika squirmed quietly on Esther's lap. I thanked God for His goodness to us, for seeing us through yet another day, and for His many blessings.

Then in unison we prayed, "Now I lay me down to sleep, I pray thee, Lord, my soul to keep . . . Thank you, God, for Alisha and Darika and little baby Angelika and Mommy and Daddy. In Jesus' name, Amen."

Tucking Alisha under the covers, I smoothed back her hair and kissed her forehead. "Sleep well, Alisha." She threw her arms around my neck and I hugged her tight.

"I love you, Daddy!"

"I love you too, Alisha."

15 Milestones

—Esther

I glanced down at Alisha, who was sitting at my feet coloring quietly on her writing tablet. *She seems to grow up more every day,* I thought as I reached down to brush a stray strand of blond hair from her face. It felt a bit empty without Darika with us today, but it was also less stressful. She was teething and fussing a lot, constantly wanting to be held. She had started running a fever again the day before, so we had taken her back to Lon's house for the night in accordance with the Ronald McDonald House rules.

I glanced over at Galen, who sat beside me writing in the little black journal. "Wow, we haven't written for a whole week."

He glanced up at me. "I know. We're not very faithful about this, are we?" He went back to writing. I peered over his shoulder. *April 9—Angelika's still doing pretty well. They talked about maybe taking her off the ventilator and feeding her some . . .*

"It's exciting to think of reaching these milestones, isn't it?" I asked.

"Yes, it's encouraging to see progress," he agreed. "Somehow, getting her off the ventilator seems like one of those giant steps toward going home, doesn't it?"

"Yes, and if she accepts the feeds, that's another huge step in the right direction."

"Of course, we've got a long way to go yet. But every bit of progress is something to celebrate. We'll just have to be careful not to get ahead of ourselves. We still need to live in the present."

Around noon they switched Angelika to a nasal cannula. She was off the ventilator! It was a moment of great rejoicing for us. *You can actually see her whole mouth now,* I thought. *And it's cute.*

Just then the nurse came by. "We were able to start her on feeds this morning. She seems to be handling them quite well."

"It looks like she's making good progress today." I reached in and tenderly stroked her arm.

"It does, doesn't it? I always love to watch babies graduate to new levels." The nurse smiled. "She's over 2 pounds now—and gaining!"

The day held more than one large milestone for us, though. Our biggest surprise came later in the afternoon.

The NICU was divided into several sections. The part where Angelika had spent her first few months, known as "the big side," was a combination of several rooms with lots of babies in each one, separated only by small partitions. It was noisy and had little privacy. There were also several other sections, including one named 3-L, where each baby had its own room.

In these individual rooms, a couch or recliner was often provided as a place for parents to relax with their baby in privacy or even stay the night if they wanted. We had been put on the waiting list to be moved to 3-L, though we didn't expect to be moved there soon since many others were on the list as well.

But later that afternoon, a nurse stopped by and announced, "Angelika is off the ventilator now, so we can move her to 3-L if you want."

Galen and I exchanged surprised glances, but we did not hesitate. "That would be great," Galen said.

"All right, we'll move her over there in a little bit," the nurse said cheerfully. "You'll have more room and more privacy. Someday maybe our whole NICU will be designed like 3-L. I think it would be a lot better for both the babies and the parents," she confided. Then she left, leaving Galen and me smiling over another wonderful surprise in our day.

It worked out that Alisha got to see her little sister for the first time that day. Although it was only a glimpse on the pedway as Angelika's isolette was being moved from the big side to 3-L, it was special nonetheless.

Later as I entered the double doors to the 3-L section of the NICU, I glanced around me. The wide hall was lined with cluttered nurses' desks. At the far end, a large square patch of wall was painted purple and sported a bold-faced clock. The brown floor tiling was bordered by a curving strip of slate gray flooring, and the dim lighting reflected dully on its worn surface. The soft squeak of a nurse's shoes and the rolling of a desk chair were the only sounds we heard. *It's so quiet here,* I thought. *I certainly wouldn't have noticed those sounds over on the big side.*

I smiled as I spotted the blue recliner in Angelika's room. "A perfect place to rock our little baby," I said happily. There was one long window in the room that looked out over the pedway.

Next to the window was a bench seat long enough to stretch out on if we wanted to sleep. One wall was painted a bright blue, adding a cheery atmosphere to the room. Angelika's incubator sat in the center, and a sink, counter, and cupboards completed the space.

"Well, what does our little girl think of her new home?" I asked softly as I reached in to touch Angelika's hand. "It's nice, isn't it? So nice and quiet."

As I stood talking to her, a silver-haired nurse I hadn't met before entered the room. "Hello, I'm Len." Her hearty voice and bright eyes drew me to her. "I'm almost ready to head home for the day, but I thought I'd step in and see our new neighbor here." Len peered into the isolette. "Oh my, is she ever tiny!" she exclaimed. "Hello, little miss." As she reached in the hand holes, I noticed her work-worn hands. But I could tell instantly by the way she touched Angelika that she knew what she was doing.

"Well, you seem perky enough. I've heard you're a little fighter. I like the feisty ones. Yes, I do." Little crows' feet formed at the corners of her eyes and she chuckled.

"She's done quite well," I agreed. "We're grateful."

"We'll be seeing more of each other around here, I suspect." She gave Angelika a last gentle pat. "I'll see you tomorrow, little miss. Behave yourself while I'm away."

On a balmy day toward the end of April, I sat in the blue recliner with Angelika cradled in my arms. Looking down at her, I smiled with pleasure. She was certainly growing! She now weighed 3 pounds and her feeds had increased to 2.8 ounces per hour.

Galen sat on the window seat writing in the journal again. We had sent the girls home with his parents for the day and were enjoying time together with Angelika, a rare treat for us since one of us usually needed to be with the girls.

"Did I tell you about that meeting we're supposed to go to tonight?" Galen asked as he looked up, his pen poised in midair.

"The one about remodeling the NICU?"

"Yes. I guess they want to give the whole thing a makeover so it's all designed like 3-L. I think it's a great idea."

"What do they want from us?" I inquired curiously.

"Just our thoughts about our stay here and how we feel about the difference between the big side and 3-L. At least that's what it sounded like to me."

"Oh, did the nurse tell you they decreased the oxygen flow down to 3 liters?"

Galen nodded. "It's so exciting to see the progress she's been making."

I looked down at Angelika again. She had been sleeping soundly, but now she stirred and opened her eyes. They were brown like Galen's and becoming more expressive every day. "Did you hear them talking about laser surgery for her eyes the other day?" I asked, looking up.

"Yes. I talked to the doctor who'll be doing the surgery."

"It's a pretty simple surgery, I think," I said with a catch of anxiety in my voice.

"They say there isn't much to it," Galen responded. "It's done at the bedside."

I sighed. "I guess just the word *surgery* scares me anymore."

"I know how you feel," he sympathized. "But God has brought her through so much and He's always in control no matter what we face. Still, I'm glad this surgery won't be a major ordeal like the last one."

"So am I," I agreed heartily.

Angelika whimpered and stretched in my arms.

"How's my little sweet pea?" I crooned softly. "Did you have a good nap?" I stroked her head and she nestled against me. No feeling in the world was more precious.

16 Valley of the Shadow

—Esther

The phone rang, interrupting the early morning stillness in our room. I stirred sleepily as Galen answered. "Hello? Yes, this is Galen. The vent? Is she okay now? All right. I'll be right over. Thanks for calling."

"Who was it?" I asked as he swung his feet out of bed.

"It was the nurse practitioner. She said they had a bad spell with Angelika about a half hour ago. Her saturation levels kept dropping and she wasn't getting enough oxygen, so they had to put her back on the ventilator. Her heart rate became dangerously low, and they said she wouldn't respond to any stimulus."

"Is she all right now?" I inquired anxiously.

"I'm not sure. She's breathing since she's back on the vent, but it sounds like things are pretty rough. I think one of us should go over right away."

"You can go," I said. "I should call my mom and dad and

see if they can come and stay with the girls."

"That's a good idea," he said, fumbling with the last button on his shirt and reaching for his shoes. "Can you call the prayer chains too?"

"Yes, I'll do that," I agreed.

"I'll be in touch," he called back over his shoulder as he left the room.

Tears started to my eyes as I thought about the implications of what Angelika was facing. After all the progress she'd been making, it was an unexpected blow. Wiping my eyes, I dialed my parents' number.

"Good morning, Mom. This is Esther. Angelika had a bad spell this morning. Are you busy today? . . . We were wondering if you might be willing to do that . . . Oh, thanks. That works out perfectly. We'll see you then."

My hand trembled a little as I dialed our minister's number. It was such a relief just to know Mom was on her way to be with us. A couple of my sister Leona's children were staying with my parents in Summersville, and Mom had been planning to take them back home to Indiana today anyway. So she offered to take the girls along with her and leave them at Lon and Leona's place for us. It was good to know that detail was taken care of.

"Good morning. Is this Velma?" The soft voice of our minister's wife answered in the affirmative. "We're facing a crisis here . . ."

When I had finished making the phone calls, I busied myself with getting ready for the day. My hands shook as I pushed hairpins into place and pinned on my covering. What was wrong with Angelika? Why this spell all of a sudden? I caught my eyes in the mirror and noted the worry lines. Uneasily, I turned away and tried to pray as I tidied up the room and laid out clothes for the girls. Worry dogged my footsteps as I waited for Galen's call.

I was in the middle of dressing Alisha when he called. "Hello? Yes, honey, how is she?"

Just hearing his quiet voice reassured me. "She opened her eyes when I walked in the room. Len said she hadn't opened them all morning." I felt the tension inside me slip away slightly as he continued. "She's got a good grip on my finger too, but she's in pretty tough shape. You called the prayer chains, right?"

"Yes, and Mom is on her way. She'll be here in a couple hours."

"Okay, good. I'll come back after a little bit."

I took a deep breath as I hung up the phone, trying to release some of the pent-up tension of the last hour.

"Was that Daddy, Mama?" Alisha asked curiously.

"Yes, sweetheart, that was Daddy. He's over with baby Angelika."

"Oh." She bounced down from the bed where I had just finished zipping her dress up and ran to the window. I watched her for a moment. As she stood on tiptoe to peer out onto the city below, the May sunshine streaming in the window formed a halo of gold about her head. Each child was a treasure, but they seemed even more precious in moments like these.

A whimper from the bed drew my attention to Darika. She was struggling to sit up in a mound of blankets. "How's my baby this morning?" I asked with forced cheerfulness as I picked her up. She cuddled against me, her solid little body somehow calming me as I held her close for an instant.

"Should we get ready for the day now? Alisha, bring me the brush and I'll fix your hair."

When my mom arrived, the girls were excited to see her as well as their cousins. Alisha chattered with her cousins while Galen and I talked things over with Mom. A little before noon, we said goodbye to the girls and saw them off. Then we headed back to the hospital together.

As we entered the room, the older nurse on duty looked up and greeted us quietly.

"How is she by now?" Galen asked.

"She's a pretty sick little girl," the nurse replied soberly. "The blood tests showed Staphylococcus aureus bacteria in the bloodstream. A staph infection is nothing to fool around with. But we are doing all we can for her."

Her words were less than comforting. As I stood looking down at the listless form, I felt weighted with discouragement. It was hard to see her back on the ventilator again, and the thought of the silent and deadly infection that raged in her little body weighed on my heart.

Through the afternoon hours we kept our vigil. Things did not improve, and we prayed earnestly for God to intervene on our behalf. Galen stepped out to check his text messages several times. People called to check on us throughout the day, and we felt cared for.

One of the times he was out, I sat by Angelika's bed in the blue recliner, watching her. I could see on the monitor that her heart rate was low. A moment later a young nurse came in to check on her, and almost immediately she called another nurse to come in and help her. They consulted in low tones as they worked, and I knew something wasn't right. My heart did a somersault when I heard the older nurse say, "I can't get a pulse." Though her voice was controlled, I could hear the strain in her tone. In a whirlwind of seconds, they had called in the doctors and the respiratory therapist. Time seemed to stop as the white coats surrounded the bed in a battle for life.

As we entered the valley of the shadow once again, I prayed that God would have mercy on us and spare Angelika if He was willing. "Please, Lord. She's come so far. Don't let her die. Please, God."

When Galen entered the room several moments later, his face registered surprise and then concern. "What's going on?" he asked.

"They can't seem to find a pulse." My words were hardly above a whisper. Together we prayed silently until one of the doctors came over to talk to us.

"We've got her going again," she said with relief. "She's given you more than one scare today, hasn't she?" She shook her head. "Hopefully she'll be okay now."

Her words didn't sound convincing.

Toward evening, Angelika's heart rate skyrocketed to above 200. "Tachycardia," the doctor said. "It's the opposite of what happened this morning. She's in pain too. We'll give her some fentanyl, which should help to control the pain and bring the heart rate down."

When we went to get some supper, Ben and Liz joined us. They were nearly ready to take their baby home, and we were going to miss them. "How's your little gal tonight?" Ben inquired.

"She's still pretty sick," Galen responded. "They gave her some meds to cut the pain and bring her heart rate down."

Ben nodded sympathetically, and Liz gave me a hug. "We

sure hope and pray she'll be better soon."

After supper, they stayed with us for a bit before we returned to Angelika's room.

"So how do you feel about taking Dakota home soon?" Galen asked them as we stood in the hallway.

"It feels a bit scary, but we are so ready to go home. Someday after you're home we'll have to get together so Dakota and Angelika can run around and play together." Ben grinned at the thought.

In that moment, I felt dubious that we'd ever see his suggestion become reality. Angelika seemed so low, and I had very little confidence that she would live. My emotions pressed down on my heart and almost made it hard to breathe. Deep down I knew God was in control, but this valley was very dark.

As we prepared to leave Angelika's room around 10:00 that night, Icy walked in. "Can we pray together before you go?" she asked.

"Let's do that," Galen agreed.

Circling the bed, we bowed our heads. Icy prayed first, her soft voice entreating God for us and Angelika.

"Lord Jesus, we know that you are in control and that you love us no matter what. We give Angelika to you and we trust you to do whatever is best for her. Give Galen and Esther your peace. Hold Angelika near to your heart."

Liquid emotion trembled on my closed eyelashes as I prayed aloud, giving my fear to my heavenly Father and committing Angelika to His all-knowing care. Galen prayed fervently that we would trust God's heart, whatever happened.

As I opened my eyes, they met Icy's soft brown ones, and I saw tears standing in their gentle depths. "Thank you."

Life's fragility made Angelika all the more precious.

We held each moment a treasured gift.

Who ever dreamed a baby could be this tiny! Note the pen for size comparison.

Our home away from home during our six-month hospital stay.

Creativity and family routines helped us survive.

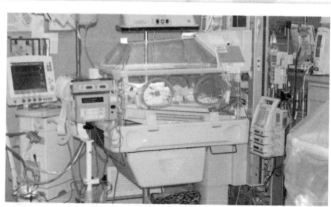

Angelika's world for those first 7½ precarious weeks.

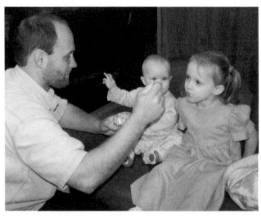

Daddy turning waiting room moments into sweet sundae memories.

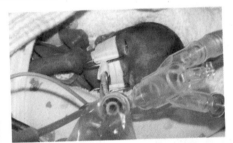

Peekaboo world! Angelika's eyes opening at around 4 weeks.

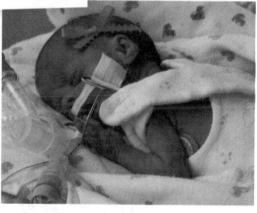

Our sleeping beauty (5 weeks, 1 lb. 11 oz.).

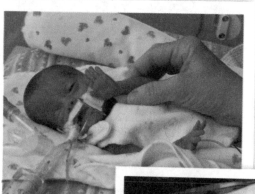

Five weeks old,
wave to Daddy!

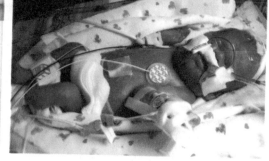

Just after emergency surgery—very swollen
from fluid retention (6 weeks, 2 lbs. 1 oz.).

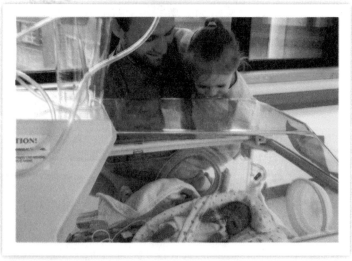

Alisha sees her little sister for the first time.

A day at the zoo.

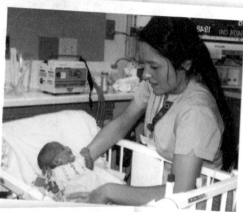

"Sweet dreams,
Angelika."
(15 weeks).

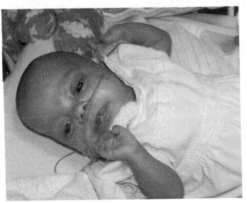

Our precious little princess just keeps
growing!

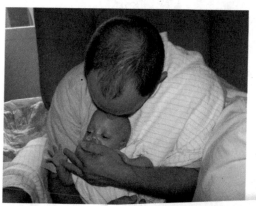

Cuddling with Daddy—he loves his girls!

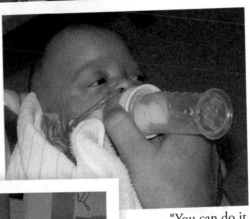

"You can do it, Angelika!" It took lots of patience and effort to get her to eat.

One of our many wonderful nurses, Icy, nurturing Angelika.

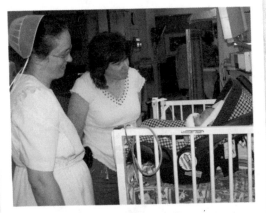

Going home day! Saying goodbye to our nurse practitioner during the car seat test.

With GOD everything is possible.

Our miracle baby. A nurse gave this stuffed flower to Angelika.

Signing release papers.

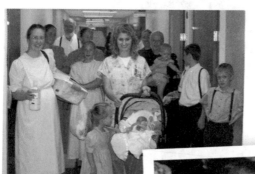

We're going home today!
August 8, 2008

Happy sisters. Angelika at 7 months.
September 18, 2008

The Lengacher family, June 2012:
Esther, Angelika, Alisha, Darika, and Galen

Angelika
(4 years old).

The words squeezed past the lump in my throat.

"She's in God's hands," Icy said simply. I knew that an "angel in skin" would be caring for my baby that night.

And then God performed another miracle. Within a week, Angelika healed from her staph infection. We couldn't stop praising God for her amazing recovery.

17 A Place of Tears

—*Galen*

I had just come back from visiting Angelika early one morning when I met Ben in the hall. "Did you hear the ruckus last night?" he asked soberly.

I shook my head. "No, what was going on?"

"You know John and Mandy, that young couple who also has a baby over in the NICU?"

When I nodded, he continued, "Their room is right next to ours, and last night those two just went all out. It was awful to hear how they fought. I've heard them fight before, but last night was really bad—so bad that the manager came and kicked John out. They told him he can't come back anymore. They're letting Mandy stay for now, though."

I shook my head sadly. "That's too bad. They aren't even married, are they?"

"No." He shrugged. As I climbed the stairs to our floor, I thought of John and Mandy's situation. I kept my eyes open for an opportunity to talk with John.

As I entered our room, Alisha ran to me. Darika crawled behind her, trying to keep up. "Good morning, Alisha. Did you sleep well?" I reached down and tousled her hair as she wrapped her small arms around my leg. She nodded and hid her face against me, pretending to be shy. Darika had arrived by now and was trying to pull herself up too. When I picked her up, she pointed across the room and grunted.

Esther laughed. "She's trying to talk more and more these days, communicating any way she can."

I grinned. "Are you a big girl now, Darika? All grown up?" Alisha tugged at my hand to remind me she was still there, and I laughed. "You're growing up too, aren't you? Pretty soon we'll have big girls instead of babies."

"I am a big girl," Alisha declared somberly.

"That's right, you are a big girl, and you're a big helper too! Well, Mama, how about some breakfast?"

Between helping the girls with their meal and eating a few bites ourselves, I told Esther about John and Mandy.

"Last time I heard, their baby wasn't doing very well," Esther told me. "I can't imagine all the stress this would put on a couple who doesn't know the Lord and are unmarried besides. I don't wonder that they're struggling."

"I'd like to talk with John if I get the chance," I responded. "Maybe I can share a bit of hope with him and at least let him know that we care about what they are going through."

"That's a good idea. I wonder how Mandy will make it here alone."

"I don't know. But I think we should pray for them."

"Definitely," Esther agreed.

My chance to talk to John came later that same day. I

spied him leaning against his car talking on his cell phone when I drove into the parking lot across from the Ronald McDonald House. Just as I was passing him, he finished his conversation and I stopped to talk to him. "Hi, John, I'm Galen Lengacher." I held out my hand and he shook it.

"Hello. You stay at the Ronald McDonald House?" His young, handsome face was impassive, but his dark eyes held a hint of questioning, as if he wondered why I was talking to him.

"Yes, we do. My wife Esther and our two little girls are staying here right now since we have a baby in the NICU."

His tone was warmer as he replied, "My girlfriend Mandy and I have a baby in there too." His voice faltered just a bit as he added, "Things aren't looking too great for us, though."

"I'm sorry to hear that. Is there anything I can do to help?" I asked.

"Naw, I guess part of it's my own fault anyhow. We had a big argument last night and they kicked me out." He seemed to be opening up, and I prayed that God would give me the right words to say to him.

"How is your baby?" I asked.

"Oh, she's still such a little squirt, and they're not giving us much hope, I guess." He scuffed his boot toe against the pavement and avoided eye contact as he added, "It's a rough life. Some days I wonder if it's worth it."

"It sounds like it's really hard for you right now," I sympathized. "We've faced a lot of ups and downs in our journey with our baby too. I don't know how we would have made it without the sustaining grace of God."

He shook his head. "I guess I'm not really a religious type

133

of person. My mom used to pray before meals when I was a kid, but I just never saw any point in it. I know there's a God and all that, but I don't think He'd have time for a guy like me."

After a pause, I looked up and he met my eyes. "John, God sees what you're facing right now, and He really does care about you. He loves you and Mandy and your baby. In fact, He loves you so much that He sent His only Son, Jesus, to die so that you could know Him personally and live a life free from sin and doubt."

He shrugged. "I don't know. Like I said, I'm not really much into that kind of stuff, but I'm glad it works for you."

"Well, John, I'll be praying for you," I told him. "And if you ever need anything, just let us know and we'd be glad to help you in whatever way we can."

He glanced up, the slightest hint of a smile lifting the corners of his mouth. "Thanks, Galen. Hope everything works out well for you too."

"Thanks, John." I turned to go with an aching heart.

How would it be to face hardship without the comfort of God's presence and the lifeline of prayer? Our situation stood out in stark contrast to John and Mandy's. Several weeks had passed since Angelika's last brush with death, but it was still fresh in my memory. I knew that the prayers of God's people had turned the tide. Earlier this week, I had written a report for our praying friends to update them on Angelika's condition and to thank them for praying for us so faithfully in our time of need.

> *5-13-08*
> *Dear Friends,*
> *We wanted to give a little update on Angelika's*

*progress so everyone knows how she is doing and how
to direct your prayers. She really has been progressing
nicely and is now 34 weeks gestational age. She weighs
3 pounds 13 ounces and is about 16 inches long.*

*Once she reaches 4 ½ pounds, they will reverse her
ileostomy. If there are no complications, we hope to
be able to bring her home within a few weeks of her
surgery. She will need to work up to full feeds, take a
bottle well, and have good weight gain to go home.*

*We want to thank everyone for all the prayers for us
and for Angelika. Also, remember to thank the Lord
for the way He has already worked.*

Sincerely,

Galen and Esther

We discovered that Mandy now had the room right next
to ours. I hoped this would afford a chance to be able to
reach out to her. One night, however, her own poor choices
caught up with her, as they had with John. She invited
some friends to her room and they had a party, which was
prohibited in the Ronald McDonald House.

They drank until they were drunk. But by the time the
police came to crash the party, Mandy had disappeared,
slipping out the back door. Later, when she returned to
her room, the manager came and gave her the verdict. Her
deadline was set. She was no longer welcome here, and she
would have to leave.

Sometime later we learned that their little girl had died,
and I was reminded once again how much this was a place
of tears. I thought how easily we could have been the ones
grieving the loss of our baby. Esther and I had shed many
tears through our journey, but God had chosen to spare

Angelika for a reason. Even through all the unknowns and ups and downs, we had been held secure by the hope that can only come from Jesus Christ. Perhaps more than anything else, that was the purpose God had in bringing us here now—that in this place of tears, those who had no hope would see His love in us and learn to know and trust the Giver of all comfort.

18 Politicians and Elephants

—Galen

May 19, 2008, was a normal Monday morning. I woke up early to visit Angelika, as I often did. When I walked in, Len was just finishing her morning routine. "How are you today?" I asked as she looked up.

"Oh, I'm just fine."

"And how about our little girl?"

"She's feisty as ever, recovering more every day from that staph infection. But her one leg is a bit swollen this morning, maybe from the way she was lying on it." I noticed that they had also moved her from the crib back to the isolette. "She wasn't keeping her heat," Len explained. "She's warmed up again now, but we'll keep her in there for a while yet."

Suddenly her eyebrows lifted. "Oh, by the way," she exclaimed, "did you hear the news?"

"What news?" I asked curiously. Len was always full of stories, and I wondered what she had to tell me this time.

"Well, because of the Kentucky primaries going on tomorrow, Michele Obama is passing through. She's stopping in southwestern Kentucky in Hopkinsville, and then she's coming to Louisville. She's coming to our hospital later today to see our smallest baby in the NICU. Then she plans to visit the kids on the seventh floor in the cancer ward." She watched my face to see how I'd receive this news.

"Well, it would be interesting to catch a glimpse of her," I replied. "I doubt we'll get to see more than that, though."

Len shrugged. "I guess I don't know why we make a big fuss over people just because they're famous, but I admit I'm looking forward to seeing her for myself. At least we can have the claim to fame that we've seen her in person," she chuckled dryly. "But I suppose you wanted to hold Angelika?"

"If she's up to it."

"Oh, I think she'll be fine. Go ahead and hold her for a while. It does these bitty kids good to be held and loved."

As I cuddled Angelika's sleepy form, I wondered with just a wee bit of excitement how the rest of the day might unfold.

When the sleek, black limousines drove up, the girls and I watched from the pedway. Michele Obama emerged with her little caravan of security and secret service personnel, made her way toward the front doors of the hospital, and disappeared from our view. "Well, that's probably all we'll see of her," I told Alisha as we headed back down the hallway.

As we came through the doors, I noticed Mary Lyn, a charge nurse, leaning against the door frame with her head bent as if she were waiting for something.

"Are you waiting for Mrs. Obama?" I asked.

"Yes, I'm supposed to take her on a tour through the NICU," she responded. "I'm just waiting for her to come up now." Her voice sounded just a bit nervous to me, but her gentle smile betrayed nothing.

"Okay, I think we'll stick around here for a little bit then." I turned with Alisha in tow and headed down the hall toward the elevators where the next potential first lady would be appearing.

Settling ourselves by the vending machines right across the hall from the elevators, I glanced around and noted that the hall was nearly deserted. Most people must have thought the same thing I did when I lost sight of her on the pedway and assumed we wouldn't see any more of her. They'd gone back to their business as if nothing unusual was afoot.

After several moments, the elevator doors opened and Michele Obama herself appeared, surrounded by the others with her. She smiled and waved to those watching. Then, spying our little girls, she turned and walked toward us. I glanced down at Alisha beside me and Darika in my arms. Their eyes were watching the smiling woman walking toward us.

"Hello, how are you today?" Michele's warm voice was friendly as she stooped to eye level with Alisha, who hung back just a bit shyly. Straightening up, she smiled at Darika. "What are their names?"

"I'm holding Darika, and this is Alisha." I rested my hand on Alisha's blond head.

"How lovely. I have two girls too. Their names are Sasha and Malia." She smiled at Alisha again and patted her shoulder. "It's nice to meet you." She shook hands with each of the little girls and me before turning back to those waiting behind her. We watched her until she was again lost to view, and then we headed to the waiting room. The girls were becoming restless and needed to get down and play.

Later that evening, as I reviewed the day's events with Esther, I grinned as I recalled our encounter with Mrs. Obama. "It felt like a highlight in history," I admitted. "It's not every day you get to meet and actually talk to someone that famous."

Esther smiled and jotted the memory down in our journal for future record.

"Look!" Alisha called excitedly. She tugged at my hand to hurry me as we neared the giraffe exhibit. "Look, Daddy. It's tall!"

"That's a giraffe, Alisha. See all his spots?"

"He has a long neck." She spoke softly now, awed by this strange creature's size.

We had taken the girls to the zoo for the afternoon, and we were all thoroughly enjoying the change of scenery.

Pausing in his work, a nearby zookeeper smiled at us and came over. "We were just marveling at how tall these critters are," I explained.

His weathered face broke into a grin. "They're the tallest living mammals. They grow to be 15 to 18 feet tall. They originally come from Africa, south of the Sahara Desert. Even the babies are tall—about 6 feet tall when they are born!"

"Now that's one big baby!" I grinned.

He chuckled. "Most of their height is in their long legs

and necks."

"Yeah, they look really gangly." I glanced up at the giraffe towering above us.

"They may look awkward," he agreed, "but they're by no means slow. Those long legs enable them to run up to 30 miles an hour."

"Wow, that's pretty fast!" I exclaimed.

He nodded. "Well, I better get back to work here." He held out his hand.

"Yes, and thank you for telling us a little more about the giraffe." I shook his hand warmly. "God truly created some amazing creatures, didn't He?"

"He certainly did. Now you folks enjoy the rest of your visit." His blue eyes twinkled down at Alisha as he turned to go.

Farther on, we saw the elephants, both the Asian and African species.

"Look at their big ears, Alisha." Esther held Alisha's hand as we stood by the elephant exhibit. Darika, on my back in her carrier, began bouncing up and down excitedly as we stood watching the lumbering gray creatures amble about their enclosure. As one of them lifted his trunk and swished it aimlessly from side to side, Darika's excitement increased. Grunting and pointing, she tried to tell us just what she thought of these intriguing creatures with wrinkly skin and massive feet and ears.

I chuckled. "Do you like them, Darika? They're big, aren't they? They're called elephants."

"Is that little one a baby?" Alisha asked. I followed her pointing finger to a half-sized elephant on the far side of the enclosure.

"It looks like it. Let's see here. It says that this elephant baby was born on March 18, 2007. That means it was born just last year. His mom's name is Mikki."

Moving on, we stopped to see the rhinos and camels.

"See his big hump?" I pointed to an especially large camel. "That's the kind of animal the wise men rode when they came to visit baby Jesus. Remember?" Alisha nodded, fascinated.

After the bears and seals, the girls seemed ready for a change of pace, so we headed for the carousel. We had purchased tickets at the gate and were wondering how the girls would enjoy their ride. We were not disappointed.

As we neared the beautiful antique carousel with its colorful animals, the girls grew excited. When it was their turn to ride, Esther helped Alisha onto a big lion with a bright blue collar, his mouth opened in a half snarl. Darika's steed was a prancing black horse with a golden mane and iridescent trappings. The smiles and giggles of glee more than repaid what we had spent to purchase tickets.

The little train was our last stop before we left the zoo. The children thoroughly enjoyed their ride over the winding track and didn't want to get off when it was over.

As we left, Alisha looked up at me and asked, "Can we come back and have another train ride soon?" Esther and I exchanged smiles, glad they had enjoyed the day.

"We can probably do that sometime, Alisha. Shall we stop for ice cream on the way home?"

She nodded happily. Ice cream was a sure way to end the day well.

19 Weekend Diversion

—*Esther*

On Friday, May 30, the air was heavy with heat and humidity, like the weather before a thunderstorm. My two sisters were coming with their families, one from Lexington, Indiana, and the other from Antrim, Ohio. We were planning a picnic at the Riverfront Park that evening, and I was anticipating the evening very much. It had been a hard week, and we needed to get away and do something different for a while.

"I hope it doesn't rain," I worried aloud as we got in the van to drive over.

"Oh, I don't think it will. The chance of precipitation is pretty low," Galen comforted as he strapped Darika into her seat. "Ready to go?"

Alisha nodded vigorously.

"I think we're all pretty excited about tonight, aren't we? I certainly am." Galen grinned at me and I returned his smile.

When we arrived, Don and Lorene were already there.

Their lively children were playing a game of tag. They had seven—three boys and four girls. After unbuckling Alisha's car seat, I reached for Darika while Galen got the food and stroller from the back. Glancing toward the picnic area, I noted that Don was assembling what looked like a brand new grill in the shade of the spreading trees. It would be just like him to purchase a grill and use it on such an occasion.

"Esther, how are you?" Lorene's warm brown eyes met mine, and then I was embraced in the hearty hug of my older sister.

"I'm glad to be here! How about you?"

"Oh, we're doing well. I am so excited about this evening and the weekend. We have some catching up to do," she bubbled.

I nodded and followed her to the picnic tables under the shade where she was laying out food. "Oh, Lorene, this looks like a feast."

Laughingly, she gestured toward the children scattered across the grass at play. "It takes a lot to feed all these hungry mouths. Especially with the boys growing so much right now." I nodded, smiling agreement. "So how was this last week?" Lorene asked. "How is Angelika doing?"

I set Darika in the stroller Galen had brought and went to work beside my industrious sister. "The past week had its ups and downs," I admitted. "Several days were really hard."

"I'm sorry." Lorene looked up and her eyes were full of sympathy. "More bad news?"

"Well, they decided they should do a spinal tap. I think they were still worried because of her staph infection. On Monday morning when I was sitting by Angelika's bed, I asked the nurse how they did a spinal tap since I knew they were planning to do one later that day. She told me they bend the baby to tighten the back and provide better access to the spine, and then they stick a needle in to withdraw the spinal fluid. Hearing that was about enough to put me over the edge. I had to get up and leave."

Lorene nodded. "It's just so hard to think of our babies suffering, isn't it?"

"Yes, it's terribly hard. I went to the chapel so I could cry without having other people watching, and I just had to commit everything to the Lord again. Sometimes when Angelika has to face so much pain, I find myself asking God why. I'm almost willing to let her go in those moments if it would only end her suffering."

My voice broke, and I paused to regain my composure. "When I got back Monday afternoon, they informed me that they had tried to do a spinal tap twice and had failed both times." I sighed.

"I guess they're just humans like us trying to do their job. But when it's your own baby, I know it feels frustrating." Lorene read my thoughts and I nodded.

"Sometimes I feel so defensive, like I just want to protect Angelika from all the things they're doing to her."

I glanced up as I saw a group of people approaching. "Oh, there come Lon and Leona!"

After greetings and hugs were exchanged all around, the cousins spread out again to play, and Leona joined us at the tables as we finished laying out the supper. Don had finished setting up his grill, and Galen came over to get the hot dogs and hamburgers. "Esther, did you see the four-seater bike Don rented for the evening?" he asked. My eyes followed his pointing finger to where some of the older boys were getting on a bike with four sets of pedals and a blue-and-white striped canopy over it. "I think I'll have to take a spin later and try it out," he grinned.

"It looks like fun," I agreed.

"We were just talking about how Angelika is doing and how Esther's week went." Lorene filled Leona in.

"When you talked to me early in the week, it sounded like things were a little rough," Leona said softly. "How is our little girl now?"

"Today they did a head CT scan and found a spot on the back of her brain. They said she doesn't have much of a cerebellum, and this will probably affect both her balance and her coordination as she grows older."

"I'm sorry!" Lorene exclaimed softly. "I imagine that was hard news to take."

Leona reached out and put a gentle hand on my shoulder. "God has worked so many miracles for you already. It's certainly not beyond Him to work another one."

"That's what Galen said too," I agreed. "I just need to keep being reminded that God is in control. He has been very good to us through this whole thing, and I know He's working in Galen and me too. He won't waste the experience, even though it feels so hard sometimes."

Our conversation turned to other things as we shared about our lives, our children, and our marriages. It felt so good to be with my sisters again!

Suddenly Don and Lorene's son Landon shouted, "Look, there comes a big boat!" All the children paused in their play to look toward the river, and the men paused in their talk. There was a scramble as they raced to watch the big barge churning the smooth waters of the Ohio River as it passed.

"The boats will provide good entertainment all evening," Lorene chuckled as a smaller fishing vessel trolled into view.

"Our girls love to watch the boats when we come here," I agreed.

After an evening of relaxation and seeing some fireworks across the river, we packed up to go home, our hearts filled with the love of family.

We made the most of our weekend. Don and Lorene's family went home with Lon and Leona that night and then returned the next day to spend more time with us and Angelika. My mom and dad joined us for part of the day as well. "We'll be back again tomorrow," Don promised as we parted that afternoon.

"We can have a church service in the chapel and grill in the park for lunch if you want," Galen suggested.

"That sounds good," Don agreed.

As we filed into the chapel the next morning, I remembered the first service we'd had here when Angelika was just born. Again we settled into the blue chairs, and Galen opened with prayer.

"Thank you, Lord, for family and for the gift of time away," I prayed silently as I thought of how refreshing the weekend had been.

For a while we blended our voices in songs of praise and worship. Then we shared Scripture verses from memory.

" 'The LORD is my strength and song, and he is become my salvation: he is my God, and I will prepare him an habitation; my father's God, and I will exalt him.' Exodus 15:2," Don began.

147

"Psalm 103:2-4: 'Bless the LORD, O my soul, and forget not all his benefits: who forgiveth all thine iniquities; who healeth all thy diseases; who redeemeth thy life from destruction; who crowneth thee with lovingkindness and tender mercies,' " Galen quoted. "We've been given so many good things to be thankful for."

"'The eternal God is thy refuge, and underneath are the everlasting arms.' Deuteronomy 33:27," Lorene added.

"That has been a very special verse to us through this journey, especially early on," Galen said. "It's so good to know He's always there. Let's sing 'Great Is Thy Faithfulness.' "

As our voices blended in the familiar words of the hymn, I was reminded again of how faithful God had been through this difficult journey. He had also shown me that He cared about the small details of our lives through all the special touches He had added to this weekend. In His strength we would go on. In the good times and the hard times, He would continue to be faithful.

20 Bulldog With a Bone

—Esther

I moved quietly in the slightly darkened room, talking softly to Angelika as I prepared her bath. When I had arrived that morning, the nurse had asked me if I wanted to bathe her. I agreed eagerly. It would be the first bath I'd ever given her.

As I lifted her into the water, I noted how big she was getting. "Our baby girl is growing up," I cooed. "Yes, you are." Her big eyes met mine trustingly. "You're almost 7 pounds now, big girl. Just about ready to go home."

Tomorrow was June 15—her due date. That had been our mental milestone for our anticipated home-going, but it looked as though we needed more patience. Angelika had to have another surgery before we could think of taking her home.

For some time now, Galen had been asking repeatedly for a surgery date. One of the nurse practitioners had jokingly compared him to a bulldog with a bone. We had both laughed at this illustration, but it was true. Since we couldn't even consider going home until after this last surgery to reverse her ileostomy, we were eager to have it completed. The next day we had finally gotten a surgery date: June 18. We had breathed a great sigh of relief.

"Sweet pea, do you like the water?" I gently swished the warm liquid over her. She whimpered a little. "It's okay. Mama has you, Angelika." I lifted her from the little plastic tub and wrapped her in a towel. "There, we're all clean now. Good girl, Angelika. You were good for Mama, weren't you?" I kissed the top of her smooth head and held her close for a brief instant before dressing her. She had become so precious to us. As she became more responsive and less fragile, we treasured the greater freedom in caring for and cuddling her.

Wednesday morning I awoke with a start. I turned over sleepily to look at the bed next to ours, but the girls were not there. Then I remembered that we had sent them with my sister Leona the night before because Angelika was to have her surgery done today. Funny how I still missed them even when they were just gone for a single night.

As the reality seeped into my still-foggy brain, anticipation mingled with apprehension. It would be so good to get this surgery over with. Maybe soon we could go home! But still, surgery always carried a risk. Even though Angelika was bigger now and the risk was reduced, the memory of former surgeries and the close calls afterward brought back a familiar prickle of fear. "Lord, please keep our little girl safe again today," I prayed. "She's in your hands, and I know she's safe there. Help me to trust you and be at peace.

And guide the surgeon's hands, Lord. Please let the surgery go well and help her to heal quickly so we can go home. But, Lord, help us to be faithful as long as you ask us to stay here."

Holding Angelika before she went to surgery, I traced the features of her delicate face again and again, imprinting them on my memory—the button nose, expressive brown eyes, and the hint of a double chin line. Her skin was still olive brown but had mellowed from the nearly black look of the early days. Her dark eyebrows were becoming more distinct as well. I held her hand in mine and noted that, although her slender wrists and arms looked fragile, her grip was strong.

"They gave her blood yesterday to make sure she's in good shape for today. I have high hopes that this surgery will go smoothly," Galen spoke from where he stood behind my shoulder.

I nodded. "She's older now too. That should help."

When the nurse came to get Angelika, I relinquished her grudgingly. We followed them to the holding room where I was allowed to hold her again until they were ready to take her into surgery. Then Galen and I made our way to the waiting room.

The waiting room was relatively empty except for another couple who seemed lost in the magazine and newspaper they were reading. Galen and I talked little. I watched the clock on the far wall and prayed. Slowly the first hour slipped by. My mind wandered back to when we had said goodbye to Ben and Liz. I was so glad for them that they had been able to go home, but we missed their cheerful friendship. That day had felt especially hard as we thought about how far off our own home-going seemed. Maybe now if all went well with this surgery . . . My thought blurred as I nodded off. Both Galen and I were drowsy after a late night and an early morning.

An hour and a half later, the surgeon came in. "Things went well," he announced cheerfully. "Her bowel is back in place and we repaired the hernia. We've moved her back to 3-L for recovery, and you can go in and see her any time now." We were both on our feet as he finished, and we followed him from the room.

Angelika was drowsy. After a little while, she opened her eyes and looked at us dazedly before shutting them again. When we left to get a bite to eat, she seemed to be doing well. We felt relieved that things had gone so smoothly.

That afternoon, though, as we watched by her bedside again, her breathing became rapid and she tossed restlessly. Almost instantly she was surrounded by doctors and nurses. Their conversation was low, their sentences short and clipped. We knew things were urgent. We began to pray silently and earnestly.

I caught a glimpse of her face through the bustle of white coats coming and going. It was tinged blue with lack of oxygen, and her breathing was quick and labored. A doctor with a worried look in his gentle eyes came over to us to explain what was happening.

"Her lungs have collapsed," he said quietly. "It's called spontaneous pneumothorax. Her lungs are going into spasms because of the pain meds, which is causing the shortness of breath, rapid heart rate, and the pain she's experiencing. We're doing all we can for her, and we hope to have everything under control shortly." He turned back to her bedside, and we bowed our heads together and continued praying.

The crisis passed. Angelika's condition stabilized and we breathed easier again, though we continued to pray for God's hand of protection and healing on our little one. She was still restless when we left her that night, but seemed to be relaxing a little.

The next day my brother Leroy and his family came to spend the day. My parents stopped by as well. It was comforting to be surrounded by the love and security of family after the trauma of the day before. The girls were back with us too, and caring for them helped take away my anxious thoughts.

That morning there were several cards in the mail. One of them was from a couple in our church. The little wren on the light green card reminded me of Jesus' words recorded in Matthew that talk about how God cares even for unimportant sparrows.

The words penned inside reminded us that God's people were holding us up in prayer. "May God continue to be with you each day, granting you grace, strength, and patience. We are praying for you and share in your joy of Angelika's continued progress."

Angelika was restless for several days. By the weekend, though, things were looking better. On the way to church, I scribbled an update for all those who had been praying over the time of her surgery. We had felt their prayers throughout those days as we watched God intervene again in sparing the life of our little girl.

Thanks for praying for me again as I had surgery on Wednesday, June 18. They reversed my ileostomy, which means my bowels will be functioning normally again. There is much danger of infection, so please continue to pray for my health.

I also need you to pray that I could take bottle feedings in a few days. The doctor says I really need to take the bottle.

God bless you all,
Angelika

As I watched the rolling countryside slipping past the window. I turned my mind to the church service ahead. We would be there soon. My heart lifted at the thought. It was always a blessing to worship with our church family, and we had much to praise God for this Sunday!

21 Trip of the Lost Luggage

—Galen

It was late June. After eating breakfast at the Ronald McDonald House, we headed for home because we needed to do some errands. Several things needed to get done before our upcoming trip to Georgia for my nephew Caleb's wedding.

At home, I checked the chicken houses to make sure they were in good running order. Then I mowed the yard, and Alisha and Darika took turns riding with me. Esther sprayed the rose plants and ferns, since she noticed that beetles had been taking over.

When we got back to the hospital and I was sitting with Angelika, I opened the journal to see what Esther had written recently.

> *June 24, 2008—They started Angelika on Pedialyte feeds today. She seems to be doing pretty well right*

*now. They moved her into a crib again today and put
a fish mobile in her bed. A bit of soft music is calming
to her sometimes.*

*Angelika had an eye exam. Still the same. One eye
good. The other eye not completely clear.*

*June 25, 2008—Wednesday. Galen held Angelika
this morning. They turned her oxygen down to two.
Tomorrow she'll get the regular nasal cannula. She's
getting milk for the first time since her surgery.*

I closed the journal and got up to take a last look at
Angelika sleeping peacefully in her crib before I left for the
night. The lashes resting on her thin cheeks fluttered just a
little as I reached down to comfort her. Resting my hand
on her arm, I spoke soothingly, "Sleep well, little one." She
sighed and nestled close to my hand, sensing my presence.
I brushed my finger softly across her cheek. "We love you,"
I whispered. Her breathing slowed as she settled back into
a deeper sleep. Several moments later I slipped away. It had
been a long week, and I was ready for some sleep myself.

✿ ✿ ✿

I awoke early on July 4 with one thought uppermost in my
mind. Today was the day for our flight to Georgia. Wasting
no time, I rose and dressed. I wanted to see Angelika one
more time before we left. Esther was awake and just getting
out of bed as I left the room several minutes later.

When I arrived, Angelika was wide awake. Her brown
eyes met mine as I stepped up beside the crib. "Good
morning, Angelika," I greeted her cheerfully. "How did our

princess sleep?" She smiled at me and I playfully tickled her chin. "You woke up on the right side of the bed, didn't you?" I grinned.

After checking with the nurse, I picked her up and sat down in the blue recliner. "Mommy and Daddy are going on a little trip," I told her gently. "But we'll be back soon, and Auntie Judith and Lorene will be here with you, so you won't get lonely." She watched my face, wide-eyed and serious, but when I smiled down at her, she smiled back. "Yes, you'll be just fine, won't you?" I cooed. "Yes, you will."

She had been learning to drink from a bottle, and we were all feeling encouraged. Though she struggled quite a bit with refluxing, she was making good progress. And every little bit of progress was a step closer to taking her home.

A half hour slipped by as I relished time with my little girl, talking and cuddling. Glancing at my watch, I was startled at how quickly the time had gone. I knew I should head back to help Esther get ready to go. Half-heartedly I rose to put her back in her crib. "Goodbye, Angelika Rose. Daddy loves you." Her eyes held mine trustingly for another moment before I patted her hand gently and turned away.

Because her awareness of when we came and went was growing as she got older, it was becoming harder to leave her alone overnight. Sometimes she gripped our hand when we were telling her goodbye, as if telling us not to leave her. Eventually we decided that I would sleep in her room sometimes so she wouldn't feel alone, while Esther stayed with Alisha and Darika.

As she got older, we could be more involved with her care, which added to our desire to be with her more. It would be good practice for when we took her home.

As I entered our apartment, Alisha met me at the door.

Exuberantly, she announced, "Mama said today is the day we are going to fly on the big airplane, Daddy!"

I tousled her sleep-wild hair and laughed. "That's right, Alisha. You've been waiting for this for a long time, haven't you?"

Esther's brother James dropped off his wife Judith and their oldest daughter Brittany just before we left. Lorene and her daughter Julia came a little later.

With a few last-minute instructions and hugs all around, we said a thankful goodbye and headed out to the minivan. Our luggage was stowed and we were ready for adventure.

After checking in our luggage at the airport and going through security, we made our way to the gate. The girls were both squirmy, and Alisha whispered excited questions as we waited to board our plane. "How long now, Daddy? How long till we get on the big airplane?"

Finally our zone was called. Alisha held my hand tightly as we made our way down the jet bridge. A cheerful blonde stewardess smiled down at her as we reached the plane. "Good morning, and welcome aboard."

We found our seats and settled in for the flight ahead. Soon we were taxiing down the runway, and then with a roar of engines, the jet lifted off and we soared skyward. Glancing down at Alisha, I watched her wide eyes and smiled reassuringly. "It's fun, isn't it?" She nodded and gazed out the window with wonder at the swirling cloud banks outside that now obscured any view of the city below us. I tried to imagine what she must be feeling as the plane wings dipped and we circled higher, gaining altitude before leveling off into steady flight.

When we arrived at the Atlanta International Airport just

over an hour later, we set off in search of our luggage. After some time, we began to realize just how big the Atlanta airport was. Seeing the train, or the automated people mover, we decided to take it to baggage claim.

When we got there, a disappointment awaited us. Our luggage was nowhere in sight. After a bit of waiting, I left Esther and the girls to watch for it while I headed for the car rental counters. When I returned some time later, the luggage still wasn't there and the girls were growing restless. "What are we going to do?" Esther asked anxiously. "Do you think it's lost?"

I shrugged with growing concern. "It's hard telling. It might be." When we inquired after our luggage, personnel apologized but told us there was nothing they could do. We resigned ourselves to waiting, just in case the luggage had come in on the plane but had somehow been missed.

After an hour of waiting, we gave up. Wondering what we would wear to the wedding the next day, we drove through the July heat toward Montezuma. All the dresses Esther had sewed for herself and the girls were in those missing suitcases, as well as my own dress clothes.

Pulling into a Walmart parking lot along the way, we decided we'd pick up clothes for me since I was to be an usher in the wedding the next day. "I'm not sure what we'll wear," Esther worried. "It looks almost hopeless that we'll get our luggage in time."

"Maybe one of the church ladies would have a dress to spare," I suggested.

"Yes, they might," she said dubiously.

"Why don't you call our folks and let them know what happened?" I suggested. "It will give them time to find something in time for tomorrow yet." She did, and they kindly assured her that they'd do their best to find suitable clothes for both Esther and the girls. Now, even if the luggage didn't show up, we would be able to make do.

We went straight to the church for the rehearsal that evening. Watching Caleb and Leronda together brought back fond memories of our own wedding eight years before. I smiled as I watched their happy faces.

Just as we were leaving Leronda's parents' house after a delicious pizza supper, we received a call notifying us that our luggage had been located. I took off and drove the two hours back to the airport to collect the lost luggage. The whole situation seemed almost laughable.

We were up with the sun the next morning and arrived at the church house by 7:30 in time for pictures. The day went well and the wedding was lovely. You'd think no couple had ever been happier than Caleb and Leronda as they were pronounced man and wife, their faces radiant with the joy of first love.

Everything from there on was a bit of a blur as we said our goodbyes, packed up, drove to the airport, and returned our rental car, all in time to catch our flight back home that evening. Before I fell asleep late that night, my last thought was that we could accurately classify this as a flying trip.

22 Setbacks

—Esther

"I think you will probably be able to go home by the first of August if all continues to go well." The nurse practitioner had just finished an evaluation of Angelika's condition and was giving us her prognosis. I did some quick mental math. *It's July 10 today, and there are 31 days in July. That means that it will be 21 days yet.* My heart sank a little. It was still nearly a month away.

When the nurse practitioner had gone, I looked over at Galen. "Do you think they'll be right this time?" I asked a bit skeptically.

He shrugged. "They were wrong last time, but we will go home someday. We know that much at least." He grinned wryly. "It feels as though it will never come, doesn't it?"

I sighed. "Sometimes I feel as if time has stopped and we're stuck right here. I almost despair of ever going home." I looked down at Angelika resting in her crib. "But I know it's coming sometime. It has to."

"That's right. We need to focus on one day at a time. The end of the race is often the hardest part, and the greatest test of endurance comes when you're almost to the finish line. I just pray we'll be faithful as long as God wants us here."

I nodded. "I know. That's really what I want too. But it just feels so hard in the middle of it. I've been feeling more concerned lately, since they've been moving more MRSA cases to 3-L."

"That really bothers me too. I talked to the head nurse about it. She said they're using 3-L because they're overcrowded in the big side of the NICU and they need an isolation ward for the babies that have the MRSA infections. 3-L is the best solution they feel they can come up with right now."

"I don't see how they can feel good about it, though," I countered. "MRSA is highly contagious, and they put all the healthy babies at risk whenever they bring an infected case into this environment."

"I know. Len was telling me the other day that the strain of staph bacteria that causes MRSA is highly resistant to the antibiotics that they use to treat ordinary staph infections. After our scare with Angelika's staph infection, I don't want to touch anything like it with a ten-foot pole. But we really can't do anything about it right now. We'll just have to pray for protection and keep protesting whenever we have the chance."

Several days later our worst fears were realized. A white-coated doctor informed us that our baby had tested positive for the dreaded MRSA infection.

When he left, Galen shook his head in frustration. "I guess it's just one of those times we'll have to live with the results of someone else's poor choices, but it sure doesn't seem pleasant when it's your child who has to suffer."

I brushed away a tear. "I don't know why they couldn't just listen to us. It would have saved so much trouble. Angelika has been through so much already. She didn't need one more thing. Plus, how is this going to affect the date of her discharge? It's just one more setback that will make our stay drag out longer."

"I guess the only thing to do is forgive others and trust the Lord, even though we feel upset by this," Galen said. "Let's spend some time praying and commit it to the Lord. He knows what's going on right now and how frustrated and helpless we feel."

The next day we were again approached by one of the doctors. I imagined she had bad news for us, and I felt my heart skip a beat as she came up to talk to us.

But to my surprise she announced briskly, "We have good news for you."

I felt my heart skip another beat, this time in anticipation. Could it be possible?

"We re-ran blood tests this morning, and the cultures came back negative. Angelika does not have MRSA." Though her tone and manner were businesslike, I could sense relief in her words.

"Thank you," Galen said simply, his tone embodying everything I felt—an enormous sense of relief and gratitude to God for intervening on our behalf.

✿ ✿ ✿

Time continued to drag by. There were weeks I didn't write in our journal at all, because it felt as though nothing significant had happened. However, there were days of progress too, and no matter how slow it seemed, we were always grateful.

July 19 was one of those progress days. Angelika came off oxygen. That same day the nurse tried putting her in a baby swing for a while.

"Do you like it, sweet girl?" I cooed as I sat nearby, watching her swing gently back and forth. She dozed lightly and I could tell she was relaxed. This was a day of victory. At last she was breathing on her own! One more milestone reached—one large step nearer to our goal.

But there were still more setbacks to come. The following Monday, July 21, Angelika's weight dropped and her stools became watery. She had to have a PICC line put in to supply her with fluids. This special kind of IV would be able to stay in longer than a regular one and would allow for better management of her medication and nutrition. It would also allow her blood to be drawn without repeated poking.

That evening Galen took the girls to the park while I spent time with Angelika. As I sat beside her bed and watched her toss and turn in discomfort, I felt like crying. "Lord, will she ever be well?" I asked. "Will we ever get to go home?" I felt despair seeping through me. "Lord, it feels as though we've been here for years. I know your plans are perfect, but sometimes I wonder if this valley will ever end."

Angelika fussed fretfully and I reached out to comfort her. "It's okay, Angelika. Mama's here." In that moment a picture formed in my mind of how God comforted me. I could not remove Angelika's pain, but I could be there to hold her hand and comfort her with my presence. So, too, God was with me in this moment of pain. Though He had chosen not to remove what was causing the pain, He was here. As my heart cried out, I felt Him draw near to strengthen and comfort me. He assured me that there would be enough grace for today and for every day following, as there had always been before. After all, hadn't He intervened on our behalf time and again?

"They have cottage meetings tonight, don't they?" I asked glumly as we drove back to Louisville after church one Sunday afternoon.

"Yup. Why, are you feeling the Sunday blues again?" Galen glanced over at me sympathetically.

"I guess so. It just feels so hard to be coming back here while everyone else goes on with their normal lives," I admitted.

"Yeah, every time we hit this ramp coming off the interstate, I feel the same way." Galen concentrated on the road ahead as he maneuvered through busy traffic. "It's like a wave of self-pity washes over you before you even know what's happening."

"I know. I guess we just need to focus on what we have to be thankful for. At least we got to go to church this morning."

"Who knows, maybe someone will show up for a visit yet tonight." Galen tried to sound cheerful.

I didn't reply. Except for family, visitors had become scarcer now that things were winding down for us at the hospital, and I rather doubted anyone would show up.

After a pause, Galen changed the subject. "You know, we haven't suffered financially during the whole time we've been at the hospital," he remarked thoughtfully. "Our church body has been so generous and God has been so gracious."

I nodded, considering how every Sunday we had found enough money in our church mailbox to carry us through that week. "And the way He's been providing for the medical bills through so many avenues is amazing too," I added.

"I know. We've been so richly blessed and well taken care of. Even with the huge hospital bill we'll get after Angelika's discharge, I feel at peace, trusting that God will continue to take care of us. He's proved Himself so faithful through these last months."

When we arrived back at the Ronald McDonald House, Galen's phone rang. "Hello, this is Galen. . . . Hey, that would be great! We were just feeling a bit lonely up here. All right, we'll see you then. Thanks."

He hung up his phone and grinned. "That was your sister-in-law's parents. They're coming to see us this evening."

I sighed with relief as gratitude filled me. "I guess God knew we needed company. Now the evening won't seem nearly as long."

"It's just another timely reminder that He cares about us," Galen agreed.

Our predicted home-going date came and went. The temptation to become discouraged was tremendous. Still, God kept sending little bits of encouragement our way to show us that He was in control of our circumstances. The prayers of God's people also continued to uphold us, and their cards were encouraging.

So we continued to press on day by weary day, trusting that in God's time, this journey would come to an end. Sometimes we nearly gave up hope, but we knew the going-home day would come someday. So, too, our trust in God was not based on feelings, but on faith in His promises and His proven faithfulness.

23 The Long-Awaited Day

—Esther

Is today really the day? The question rang through our minds again and again that bright August morning. It was Sunday, August 24, and today was to be our home-going day. After more than six months in the hospital, we could hardly believe we were going home!

The night before, there had been some uncertainty as to whether we would get to go or not. Angelika had been vacillating on her weight, and she had to weigh a certain amount to go home. That night when Icy called with the news that she was up to the right weight, we were thrilled! The last roadblock to going home had been removed. We went to bed with a sense of mounting anticipation.

The morning dawned bright and warm, matching our spirits. Dr. Ginger confirmed our hopes by announcing, "She's going home today!" We called my parents to tell them the good news. Excited, they agreed to come up and help us move out of our room in the Ronald McDonald House that forenoon. Lon's family, who had Alisha and Darika with them, said they would come after church to drop the girls off. So everything was arranged and we went into high gear.

"It's hard to believe how much stuff a person can collect over six months," I laughed as Mom and I packed boxes. We had taken some of our things home several weeks before, but there was still a lot left to move.

"Well, it's been half a year, and it takes a lot for a family to live," Mom assured me. "It's really not that much. It just feels like a lot when you have to move it all at once."

"Are these boxes ready to go?" Dad asked, lifting a box of food supplies.

"Yes, those boxes by the door are all ready to go." I pointed to several banana boxes.

"We're going to have both vans full by the time we're done," Galen commented as he bent to pick up a box. He grinned. "At least we don't have to rent a U-Haul."

When we had finished loading everything into the vehicles, we went up to the hospital to get Angelika ready. There we went over a mound of paperwork with the nurse before loading up Angelika and her supplies.

I stood by the little white crib where Angelika was sitting alertly in her car seat. "Are you ready to go, Angelika? You're finally big enough to go home with us!" I exulted. "We won't have to say goodbye anymore, will we? The day to take you home is finally here!"

Lon's family arrived and brought the girls up to see their little sister. It was Darika's first glimpse of her, and Alisha's second. As they peered through the observation window, I watched their faces. Alisha waved to me, and I waved back and smiled.

Though I doubted that she could fully comprehend what was going on, she gazed happily at Angelika for a long time.

Then it was time to go. Our whole crew, including Lon's family and my parents, crowded into the hall as we made our way toward the elevators, the nurse carrying Angelika in her car seat. We stopped at the end of the hall for a group picture, our faces bright with the joy of the moment.

Alisha carried Angelika's bright pink and yellow flower from Icy. She held it up so Angelika could see it and tentatively reached out to touch her feet. I smiled. "You're going to be a good big sister, aren't you?" She nodded and watched the baby's face attentively as Angelika watched the flower waving above her. "With God, everything is possible." The bold green words on the center of the flower were like a banner of testimony to what God had done for Angelika.

In the parking lot we said our goodbyes. Leona gave me a strong hug. "We are so happy for you!" she rejoiced softly. "The day we thought would never come is here, and you're taking your baby home."

"I know. It feels too good to be true," I agreed.

"If you ever need anything, just let us know." Her caring eyes met mine.

"Thank you, Leona. You and Lon have been there for us in so many ways. We'll never be able to repay you."

"It was our pleasure and we'd do it again in a heartbeat," she assured me. I knew it was true.

Climbing into the van, I took my seat beside Angelika. The girls were already strapped into their car seats in the back. I turned to smile at them, and they both smiled back.

Waving, we slowly pulled away with Mom and Dad

following us. Reaching out, I took Angelika's tiny hand in mine. "Galen, it's so amazing that she's going home without any tubes or wires. No oxygen, no feeding tube. I just never dared to dream that she'd be able to come home like this. I was scared to take her home before, but now that she doesn't have any tubes, it doesn't really feel scary at all."

"I know," Galen responded. "Len was telling me last week that it's really unusual for babies like Angelika to go home without oxygen. I almost feel overwhelmed thinking about all that God has done for us. It's a miracle."

We fell silent, reveling in the joy of the moment and the goodness of our heavenly Father. Every little while I would look over at Angelika again, just to make sure she was still there. We were truly going home!

An hour and a half later, we drove in our lane. I felt a sudden weight fall away. My shoulders relaxed, and all I could think was that now we could settle in and relax in privacy with just our family.

Mom and Dad helped us unload, and Mom helped me fix a simple supper. When the dishes had been washed and they had gone home, we gathered in the living room for family worship. Galen held Darika, and Alisha cuddled next to him while I held Angelika.

"We'll read some verses from Psalm 118 tonight," Galen decided. He read the words fervently and joyfully. "I called upon the LORD in distress: the LORD answered me, and set me in a large place. . . . The LORD is my strength and song, and is become my salvation. . . . This is the LORD's doing; it is marvellous in our eyes. This is the day which the LORD hath made; we will rejoice and be glad in it.

"Angelika's homecoming is the Lord's doing and it is

marvelous in our eyes. We want to thank Him for all His goodness to us. Okay, Alisha, Darika. Let's kneel in a circle."

As we knelt in the warm glow of evening light, I felt a deep peace and an exultant joy. Looking down into Angelika's face, I smiled before closing my eyes. Galen's gentle voice led out in a prayer of praise and rejoicing.

Our journey had often seemed too hard. In the days of discouragement and tears, God's presence and the love of His people had carried us. And He had never left us or forsaken us.

As we looked to an unknown future, we knew we could simply rest in our Father's care. Even if we did not always understand His ways, they were always perfect. His love was always enough. He had worked all things together for good, and we knew He would continue to do so.

24 The Continuing Miracle

The summer sun was warm on Forrest's back as he walked to his mailbox. He wondered what would come in the mail today. Glancing out over the green countryside, he marveled at how, day after day, donations kept arriving to help cover the Lengachers' medical bills. He remembered the first days and weeks after Angelika had been born. Because he was in charge of the church's medical funds, he had been involved with the whole case from the start.

Soberly he recalled how small Angelika had been and how little hope he had felt that she would even make it those first weeks. Then as time went on and she continued to make progress, he had felt a thread of hope begin to grow. *I didn't know how in the world God was going to provide for this,* he mused. *It was all so new to me then, and I'd never faced something this big and complex before.*

But God certainly had His ways. Forrest thought back to

the work projects right here in their community. God had seemingly dropped the projects in their laps to help raise funds for the bills. The first one had started with an evening phone call from Paul Peachey.

"Forrest, we have a prospective project here that we could do as a church to raise funds for the Lengachers' medical bills." Paul was a man with an amazing number of connections and an equally amazing ability to get things done. Thus the phone call was not altogether surprising. "Can you come over and discuss it with me sometime soon?"

"Sure, I'll stop after work tomorrow."

So the two had met. One of Paul's friends wanted a steel building put up, and Paul had put in a word for the Lengachers since some of the men in their church had experience with this type of work. Being in construction himself, Forrest felt an immediate interest in the project as well.

"I'll call Sam Nisley and see what price he thinks would be fair on a project this size," Paul offered. When he called Forrest with the information, Forrest's first thought was that the price was way too high. He was quite sure they wouldn't get the job.

But they did. Within a week of working together, the men had raised over $20,000. Forrest knew it was a miracle they had landed a job that size in the area. But God wasn't through surprising them yet.

The Green County Cattlemen's Association had extra funds on hand and decided to put up a big steel building that summer. Paul caught wind of the project possibility, and this time the job was landed even more easily than the first one, since the board members knew about Angelika's case. This project brought in nearly $40,000.

Yes, God had certainly been active in this case. Forrest opened the mailbox and reached for the small stack of envelopes. *Hmmm, here's a letter all the way from Oregon,* he thought as he walked into the house. When he slit the envelope open and unfolded the note inside, he felt a jolt of amazement. The check inside was written out for $20,000!

The next envelope was from Tennessee. He was unprepared for what his eyes saw when he opened it. *Am I seeing right?* he wondered as he stared at the check nestled in the folded paper. But it was there in neat numbers: $50,000. "God, this is too good to be true," he breathed.

There was one more envelope. Forrest hardly dared think there would be any more money, but he was pleasantly surprised. Though not as large as the others, it was larger than most of the donations they usually received. *With this $10,000, that brings the total of today to $80,000,* he thought as he shook his head in wonder.

As he tried to wrap his mind around the astounding answer to prayer, he lifted his eyes and said, "God, I'm in awe. I know I've prayed often for your provision for this case, but so much in one day? It's such a miracle."

"Genevieve," he called. "You won't believe what the Lord sent in the mail today." Finding his wife in the kitchen, he held out the checks for her to see. "It's just unbelievable. It's such an answer to prayer!"

Wide-eyed, she rejoiced with him.

❈ ❈ ❈

On discharge, the hospital offered an 80-percent discount if the bill would be paid within thirty days. But with the original bill being more than a million dollars, even the discounted total was formidable. More money still needed to be raised.

Again the answer came through a lead from Paul. A friend of his knew of some surplus funds held by an organization, and by his request, access was given to the funds. So it was that a generous, interest-free loan, enough to cover the hospital bill, was granted. Through the continued generosity of God's people, the medical bills were covered and the loan repaid.

On a visit to André, the financial agent who had informed them they would never be able to pay the bills on their own, Forrest looked across the desk at the young man and grinned. "Well, André, by God's grace it looks like we're going to be able to pay these bills."

For a moment André was quiet. His eyes were thoughtful as he replied, "I just about can't believe it. It has to be a miracle, that's all I can say."

"It's only through God's provision and through the body of Christ working together that we've been able to cover the bills at all," Forrest agreed. "It really is nothing short of a miracle."

Epilogue

Galen and Esther still live in Kentucky where they continue to attend Summersville Mennonite Church and delight in raising the three girls God has given them.

Through several more brief hospital stays and a life-threatening bout of whooping cough in which Angelika had to be airlifted to the hospital, their conviction that God has a special purpose for their little girl's life has continued to grow. Aside from her few setbacks, Angelika has remained amazingly healthy and has grown into a delightful girl with a sparkling personality and disarming smile. Though naturally delayed due to her prematurity, her development so far has been nearly normal. This in itself is a miracle, and the Lengachers continue to use their story as an opportunity to testify to the goodness and power of God in their community and abroad.

Galen and Esther are also deeply grateful for the way they

saw God provide through a brotherhood of believers who stood by them throughout their long ordeal. Their heart in sharing this story is that others would be encouraged to increase their faith in God. Galen testifies, "We can still see our God today. He is a God who hears. He is a God who cares about individual people. It was because of this care that God placed us in the midst of difficult circumstances so that we might be a showcase of His grace. There's not a time I've doubted this, but I have often felt unworthy to have been so much the center of His attention."

The Lengachers are convinced that God will continue to work miracles of many sizes in the lives of those who trust Him.

About the Author

Buried somewhere deep in the pages of another book, the world around this author seems to fade away as she walks into the world of her characters and brings them alive on paper.

When she's not writing, Rachael enjoys pursuing a number of other interests including missions, photography, travel, and friendships. She also enjoys studying world history and culture, science, and nature. Residing in the lovely lake country of Northern Minnesota gives her the opportunity to see especially long winters transform into a springtime Eden.

Rachael is continually amazed and blessed to share in the lives of those she writes about. Her passion for writing continues to grow as God opens new doors of opportunity. "To be a scribe recording just one small chapter of His story as He works among His children is a huge privilege," she says. "When I write, I feel His pleasure, and it's my heart's desire that what flows from my pen would be for His glory alone."

Rachael enjoys hearing from her readers and invites you to e-mail her at ascribebytrade@gmail.com. You may also write to her in care of Christian Aid Ministries, P.O. Box 360, Berlin, Ohio, 44610.

About Christian Aid Ministries

Christian Aid Ministries was founded in 1981 as a nonprofit, tax-exempt 501(c)(3) organization. Its primary purpose is to provide a trustworthy and efficient channel for Amish, Mennonite, and other conservative Anabaptist groups and individuals to minister to physical and spiritual needs around the world. This is in response to the command to ". . . do good unto all men, especially unto them who are of the household of faith" (Galatians 6:10).

Each year, CAM supporters provide 15–20 million pounds of food, clothing, medicines, seeds, Bibles, Bible story books, and other Christian literature for needy people. Most of the aid goes to orphans and Christian families. Supporters' funds also help to clean up and rebuild for natural disaster victims, put up Gospel billboards in the

U.S., support several church-planting efforts, operate two medical clinics, and provide resources for needy families to make their own living. CAM's main purposes for providing aid are to help and encourage God's people and bring the Gospel to a lost and dying world.

CAM has staff, warehouses, and distribution networks in Romania, Moldova, Ukraine, Haiti, Nicaragua, Liberia, Israel, and Kenya. Aside from management, supervisory personnel, and bookkeeping operations, volunteers do most of the work at CAM locations. Each year, volunteers at our warehouses, field bases, Disaster Response Services projects, and other locations donate over 200,000 hours of work.

CAM's ultimate purpose is to glorify God and help enlarge His kingdom. ". . . whatsoever ye do, do all to the glory of God" (1 Corinthians 10:31).

The Way to God and Peace

We live in a world contaminated by sin. Sin is anything that goes against God's holy standards. When we do not follow the guidelines that God our Creator gave us, we are guilty of sin. Sin separates us from God, the source of life.

Since the time when the first man and woman, Adam and Eve, sinned in the Garden of Eden, sin has been universal. The Bible says that we all have "sinned and come short of the glory of God" (Romans 3:23). It also says that the natural consequence for that sin is eternal death, or punishment in an eternal hell: "Then when lust hath conceived, it bringeth forth sin: and sin, when it is finished, bringeth forth death" (James 1:15).

But we do not have to suffer eternal death in hell. God provided forgiveness for our sins through the death of His only Son, Jesus Christ. Because Jesus was perfect and without sin,

He could die in our place. "For God so loved the world that he gave his only begotten Son, that whosoever believeth in him should not perish, but have everlasting life" (John 3:16).

A sacrifice is something given to benefit someone else. It costs the giver greatly. Jesus was God's sacrifice. Jesus' death takes away the penalty of sin for all those who accept this sacrifice and truly repent of their sins. To repent of sins means to be truly sorry for and turn away from the things we have done that have violated God's standards (Acts 2:38; 3:19).

Jesus died, but He did not remain dead. After three days, God's Spirit miraculously raised Him to life again. God's Spirit does something similar in us. When we receive Jesus as our sacrifice and repent of our sins, our hearts are changed. We become spiritually alive! We develop new desires and attitudes (2 Corinthians 5:17). We begin to make choices that please God (1 John 3:9). If we do fail and commit sins, we can ask God for forgiveness. "If we confess our sins, he is faithful and just to forgive us our sins, and to cleanse us from all unrighteousness" (1 John 1:9).

Once our hearts have been changed, we want to continue growing spiritually. We will be happy to let Jesus be the Master of our lives and will want to become more like Him. To do this, we must meditate on God's Word and commune with God in prayer. We will testify to others of this change by being baptized and sharing the good news of God's victory over sin and death. Fellowship with a faithful group of believers will strengthen our walk with God (1 John 1:7).